Get Life Right

A few minutes into this book can change your life forever. If you are looking for a book, found this one or received it as a gift, the solution or idea you need most right now is in your hands. Find it in the Table below.

If You Found This Book

This book was placed here for people to find, enjoy, share and benefit from, as a thank you from someone whose life has been touched by it.

This book is dedicated to

Dianne

my best friend, fan, collaborator and wife

who took exquisite care

of our family while I was having my

way with these words.

Introduction

You have more potential than you can discover. Whether you are polishing up your act or you need a complete makeover, these principles, philosophies and ideas will give you the tools you need to craft your life to its fullest.

By striving to escape the boundaries of your current thinking and to become all you can be, you receive all the blessings you were sent here to enjoy and share. You become confident in your ability to create a fulfilling life and respond well to it as it unfolds. Like the horizon, as you approach what you think is your potential, it will expand ahead of you. Oprah calls this state "The fullest expression of the person you are meant to be."

Every 5 years for 50 years, a Harvard study examined the lives of 824 participants, the majority of whom were well off. The researchers concluded that even though IRIS JOY, one of the participants, had never lived above the poverty level, she had done the best job with her life. She was thoughtful, spiritual and caring. She chose the right spouse, learned constantly, stayed fit and was a good friend to everyone. The committee in charge felt that the balance she had crafted with the ingredients of her life produced the most pleasing result.

These ideas will bring more JOY into your life. Even though these ideas are easy to grasp new thinking doesn't replace thought habits suddenly. Allow time to let them settle and revisit them often. Begin your adventure by reading the subject that interests you most.

Contents

Some of the subjects you will read will be ideal for your friends or relatives. Those items which have this symbol ✉ in or near their title can be downloaded free at getliferight.com/share

Common statements for every topic in the book which are self-limiting are restated in ways that will empower you. Improve your self-talk at

getliferight.com/skillful-thoughts.

SERIES A

Sharpen Your Thinking, Focus, Creativity and Purpose

SERIES B

Plan and Finance a Really Exciting Life Doing What you Love Best

SERIES C
Learn, Love and Get the Most Out of Your Attributes

SERIES D
Finance the Life You Want, Doing What You Like Best

SERIES H

Craft the Best Life Possible

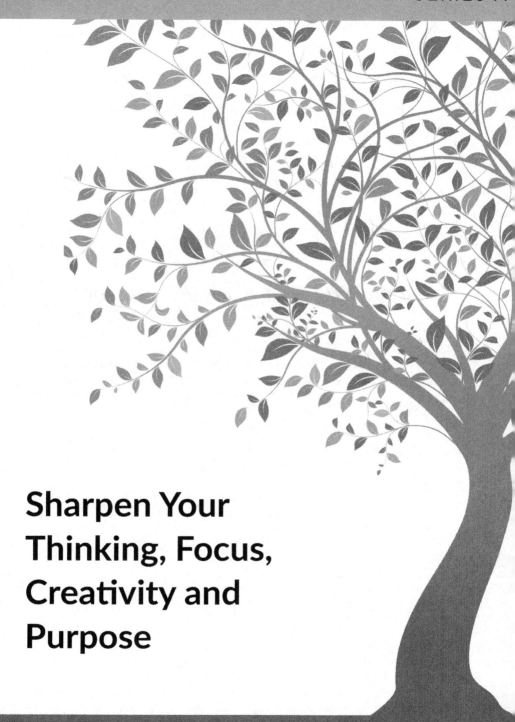

Sharpen Your Thinking, Focus, Creativity and Purpose

Make the most of all that you are.

If you are like the author, you have skipped all the front pages and plan to start here. If you go back to the table of contents and start reading the topic that will benefit you most, you will be practicing one of the ideas you'll see inside.

SERIES A: Topic 1

Get the Most Out of Your Ability to Think

A life that is right is the natural result of good thinking over time and the conscious decision to think better.

Life is 10% what happens to you and 90% how you react to it.

You react to life by telling yourself what has happened, what is happening, and what you expect will happen. Using your "self-talk," you review as many combinations of thoughts, emotions, and meanings as you think necessary. Then you choose the most appropriate ones. **The thoughts you consider and the ones you choose to go forward with are called "explanations." The explanations you choose become the programming and the rules you live by as you move forward in life.**

Your first thoughts and emotions are rarely as good as you can make them; they tend to be incomplete, shortsighted, and a little selfish. Once you process all the information and alternatives you need to make the decision into a memory, you add some notes. They state the significance of the memory and how it is likely to affect you in the future. This is called "tagging." Your tags can cause you to be afraid or bold, beaten or determined, sadder or wiser; or they can cause you to shrink from, or rise above, your current situation. This is where you also assign feelings such as blame, resentment or prejudices, or appreciation, love and empathy.

In many ways your tagging skills determine your outlook and your happiness. Choosing tags which favor long-term outcomes and calm, responsible emotions help you live and enjoy life more.

The life you have now is made up of the very best explanations and decisions you have been able to make so far. Improvements in your life will come from your ability to make better ones.

For any given situation, many explanations are possible. Each one produces different results. The information you have for making future decisions is contained in the explanations you have stored in your mind, including information that isn't true or that works against you. Your self-image is made up of those facts and assumptions. They create the "story" of you; your self-image acts like a container. You can grow within it, but it limits your thoughts and dreams. You have to be vigilant and imaginative to keep from having your collection of thoughts confine you.

When you aren't progressing, it's usually because you haven't been thinking about it or you have assumed you can't. You assume you have limitations that don't exist. Your assumptions are like prejudices; they keep you from seeing the other side and put you into a mental rut.

You allow your choices of alternatives to be limited because:

- You aren't looking imaginatively enough for better alternatives.
- You are using the wrong facts, or facts that are inaccurate.
- You aren't verifying the facts you use for your opinions or decisions.
- You have thought prejudices that filter out new ideas.
- You are influenced by what you want to be true.
- You allow your moods to influence your judgment.
- You are closed-minded or overly sensitive.
- You wish or need something to be true.
- You are influenced by how your peers think.
- You aren't sure of what you think.

Your mind will try to defend any explanation or emotion you have chosen, whether it is good or bad. That's what makes your present thinking hard to change.

Over time, a child will effortlessly change its term for a fuzzy worm from *calapitter* to *caterpillar*. Changing your thinking gets harder as you get older. You have more information, more pressures, and more complicated decisions to make. To keep up, you may accept the first thought that comes to mind. Thus, many of your explanations will be full of unverified facts and guesswork.

Your guesses and unexamined assumptions become the building blocks of your future and your reality.

Crafting Better Explanations

1. Seek and admit to yourself the absolute truth about your facts, emotions, and motivations.

2. Base your decisions on what you know, rather than what you presume to be true.

3. Consider as many explanations as possible.

4. Choose the course of action that best furthers your long-term plan for life.

5. Keep most of your choices open for reconsideration.

6. Assume that if you work and think hard enough, life will make what you need available to you as you proceed.

ASK YOURSELF

Right now, which area of my life needs skillful thinking most?

Does the choice I am about to make contribute to my Plan for life?

Which relationship could I improve by rethinking the way I am?

SERIES A: Topic 2

Form Better Thoughts and Decisions

Your brain has the ability to make sense out of confusion. Many people can read the following paragraph almost as fast as they could if the letters weren't jumbled. Try it and see for yourself:

> "Aoccdrnig to rscheearch at cmabrigde uinervtisy, it deosn't mttaer in waht oredr the ltteers in a wrod appaer, the olny iprmoatnt tihng is taht the frist and lsat ltteer be in the rghit pclae. The rset can be a total mses and you can sitll raed it wouthit porbelm. Tihs is bcuseae the huamn mnid deos not raed ervey lteter by istlef, but the wrod as a wlohe, and the biran fguiers it all out."

Because the human brain is so capable, it is easy to falsely assume that it always comes up with the right answers.

For just 10 seconds, look at the illustrations on this page. Then, without looking back, then read the next page.

Typically, you will see two images. Other people taking the same test will also see two images, but the two you see may not be the same two that they see.

Look again until you see four.

One can be seen as a young girl or an old lady. The other shows a cowboy or an old miner.

Just because you are positive you are right doesn't mean that someone with a different viewpoint can't also be right.

Until recent centuries, most people were sure that the sun circled the earth, but that concept didn't agree with what the astronomers saw. They kept looking for an explanation that would agree. Similar types of inquiries led to the discovery of gravity, magnetism, electricity and relativity. If you want to get ahead in life, you have to question how you currently think.

You tend to make explanations out of information you get from your peers, especially when you believe they are smarter, but your peers probably never check their facts.

It's tempting to make explanations like advertisements that tell you what you want to hear. Ads can exaggerate, tell half-truths, lie and distort the facts. You can advertise to yourself that you need a flashy car to get more respect from your friends, and miss the fact that with the same amount of money you could get the schooling you need for a better job. That would impress more people in the long run.

It takes more time to think up good explanations than bad ones. Life comes at you so fast that you can't take the time you need to form perfect explanations for everything you experience. Two guides speed up your decision making:

- A clear picture of what is right and wrong.
- A Plan for life with clear goals.

ASK YOURSELF

Do my explanations lead me toward the best outcomes possible for my life?

What do I advertise to myself that is not in my best interest?

SERIES A: Topic 3

End the Pressure and Guesswork

Your brain loves to feel in control. It craves certainty and wants to avoid risk and ongoing involvement in messy things. This helps it keep as much of its capability as possible available for new demands. One way it does this is by delegating most of its chores to thought habits.

This is an important skill for your brain; but it requires you to pay attention and to be strong, especially if you are anxious or compulsive by nature. Your brain may get impatient to settle ambiguities, to eliminate unknowns or to follow the line of least resistance. It presses too hard or makes you feel inadequate. That pressure causes you to make decisions before you have all the information you need.

Unfortunately, that pressure often causes you to proceed with solutions that only ...

> ... seem okay,

> ... seem to be the favorite to those involved,

> ... seem to put the matter to rest,

> ... give you a reward you've been longing for or

> ... seem to eliminate a threat (real or imagined).

All of these involve guesswork, which creates sloppy thoughts and decisions.

You have hundreds of beliefs, biases and prejudices, some of which protect you and some of which don't. Some make no sense at all. Good or bad, they create the filter through which your future decisions must pass.

You show respect for yourself when you take the time you need to gather the proper information for your decisions. Feeling pressured, anxious or hurried usually comes from being insecure or overworked, or yielding to your emotional need to appear decisive, in charge or superior. Developing wisdom takes time. The extra time it takes to make cautious decisions will give you self-confidence in all parts of your life. Recovering from sloppy decisions complicates your life and slows your progress. The time and energy lost in recovering from bad decisions will usually consume more time than it would have taken to make good decisions.

Judgment calls are different. Usually the best opportunities are rare and fleeting and require you to react quickly. Quick decisions are inherently risky. Often a decision to take a risk acknowledges that there will be glitches and do-overs, but the rewards are worth the risk and turmoil. Good judgment usually comes from gathering a huge amount of knowledge in the subject matter while watching the results of others taking similar risks. Watching the opportunity get away is also a good lesson.

You tend to record only the highlights of a thought or events in memory. When you recall them, they are distorted by what you are thinking and feeling at the time.

You tend to underestimate the risk involved in what you want to do, and overestimate the risk involved in what you don't want to do, or are afraid to do. When you want something, you are influenced by its benefits. When you don't want something, all you can see are its shortcomings. The same "knight in shining armor" you couldn't wait to marry becomes a sleaze-ball when you want to divorce.

Nearly all bad decisions are the result of not having enough information or the right type of information. You lack information because:

- You don't ask for it because you don't want others to know you don't already know the essential information.
- You never think of getting the information or you don't want to put out the effort.
- You don't know how to find the information.
- You are too busy and don't want to take the time.
- You don't check out the input you get from a friend, for fear of hurting his or her feelings.
- You don't realize the benefits of accurate information or the harm of inaccurate information.

Before you proceed with what you think is right:

- Think of all the ways it could be wrong or could be improved.
- Check all your new information with authoritative sources.
- In addition to what you expect initially, look at what the long-term consequences might be.
- Look at how your decisions will affect others. Ask people

for their input before you proceed.

- Test your conclusions before you commit to them.
- Seek and welcome information that challenges your existing assumptions.

Information is at your fingertips! In seconds, Google can fill your computer screen with facts and opinions on just about any subject you could ask.

Bookstores (and libraries) have people who will help you find information on just about any subject. Many bookstores have refreshments. Go grab a coffee and a magazine. While you are reading, notice how many inquisitive minds are growing before your eyes. Your self-image will grow along with your intelligence as you read and learn.

Decisions made with inadequate information are gambles.

ASK YOURSELF

How can I learn to use computers, bookstores, libraries and mentors?

What subject excites me enough to learn about it in every way possible?

What can I learn that will help me make a better decision next time?

SERIES A: Topic 4

Explain Your Future

Your own self-talk has more power over you than any other influence because you're talking to yourself 16 hours a day.

Whether you think of yourself as capable or incapable, you are probably right. You become what you think. In the example that follows, see how clearly that point is made. In a roomful of strangers there are usually two types of people present—one who is reluctant ("I'd rather not be here"), and one who is willing ("I will make the most of it").

The reluctant person says to himself:

- "I've never been good at this."
- "No good will come from this experience."
- "I don't know how I got trapped into this."
- "These people aren't like me."
- "Everyone can see I am uncomfortable."
- "I can hardly wait to get out of here."
- "I wish I didn't have to do this."

He assumes that those present think that:

- He looks like he doesn't want to talk.
- He must be shy or doesn't belong there.
- He isn't interested in them.
- He wishes he were somewhere else.

He decides there will be no "next time" because:

- The event was not fun.
- It's better to avoid groups of people.
- He's not good with crowds.
- People avoided him.
- People don't like him.
- He doesn't want more social obligations.

The meeting turns out as he expected.

By the time he gets home, he has taught himself the following:

- He lacked courage.
- He's not good in social situations.
- He didn't like any of those people.
- None of those people liked him.
- He would be less willing to do it again.

The willing person tells herself:

- "I will be uncomfortable at first."
- "I can practice my people skills."
- "When I talk to people, they will like me."
- "People will be easy to talk to."
- "I can learn something from everyone."
- "I can make anyone feel comfortable by being a good listener."
- "Maybe I'll meet someone who is very interesting tonight."

She assumes that those present think she is interesting and enjoyable, and they'd like to see her again. She is glad to have attended. She decides that next time:

- She'll be more at ease.
- She'll seek out those with similar interests and learn from those with different experiences.
- She'll think up better questions to ask other people about the things that interest them.
- She'll help bring people who looked uncomfortable (i.e., the reluctant man) into the conversation.

The meeting turns out as she expected.

By the time she gets home, she has taught herself the following:

- She was quite capable among people she didn't know.
- She showed courage.
- She was liked by the people she met.
- She would like to see them again.
- She would be willing to go to more meetings.

ASK YOURSELF

In what way is my self-talk blocking my growth as a person?

What can I tell myself that will make me more comfortable in unfamiliar situations?

SERIES A: Topic 5

Take Charge of Your Thought Habits

You are at the controls of an instrument that has 100 billion nerve cells. Your brain makes up only 2 percent of your body weight, but it consumes 20 percent of your body's fuel and generates enough electricity to run a small computer. It's made up of 80 percent water. It has roughly 30,000 miles of nerves. By age 5, your brain is about as big as it will ever be. At that age, some children are picking up 10 new words a day.

Neurons receive instructions from the brain as electrical impulses, but between neurons there are gaps full of chemicals through which the signals must pass. Then the receiving neurons must convert the signal back into an electrical impulse to be able to use it or pass it on.

Because your brain is so busy, it delegates as many of its responsibilities to thought habits as it can.

By the time you notice information you want to record, your brain has already checked your existing explanations, facts and feelings on the matter and formed an explanation. If it is pretty sure it knows how you feel on the subject, it records the explanation quickly. If it is unsure, it guesses at the missing parts and presents you with an explanation it believes you will accept. The process is so automatic and effortless that you are probably unaware it is happening. Since the explanations your brain makes come from what you already know and feel, they always seem right, so it's easy to allow them to pass without further thought. Like a computer, however, your brain has no judgment of its own. It can't tell the difference between what is real or imagined and what is good or bad.

> **If you aren't paying attention, some of your most important decisions will also be delegated to your thought habits.**

Your subconscious mind will seek those things that make it feel good (or make it stop feeling bad). Over time, that can cause dependency, which can grow into addiction. Behaviors that receive immediate reward get reinforced the strongest. Merely talking about yourself produces pleasurable endorphins, which are rewards. Your rewards can run away with your life.

Your ego, the self-oriented part of your brain, thinks it knows you better than anything else. It has strong opinions about what you are like, what you are capable of, how to protect your feelings, and what you must do to get what you want. It thrives on the attention or admiration of others. When it becomes addictive, your pride can run away with your life.

If your expectations cause you enough anxiety you will do what-ever you have to do to deaden the pain. So your anxieties can run away with your life.

> **You are the boss of your thoughts. If you don't take charge of them, your ego, dependencies, anxieties or thought habits will run away with your life.**

To avoid losing control:

- Replace the people, places or activities that encourage destructive behaviors with constructive ones. (Head for the gym instead of the bar.)
- Avoid rituals (the breakfast donut or killing time with the home boys).
- Avoid anxiety from all sources by:
- Loving yourself the way you are.
- Lowering your expectations for where you think you should be or what you should have accomplished in life by now.
- Changing the way you think about anything that makes you anxious.
- Having a Plan for life that you love and is working.

Seek help from doctors right away for any mental or physical problems that persist.

ASK YOURSELF

Do I usually go with the first solution that comes to mind?

How can I improve the way my brain sees me?

Are any of my explanations leading me in ways that aren't good for me?

SERIES A: Topic 6

Choose Thoughts That Will Lead You

A visionary is an idealistic person who uses his creativity to imagine far-sighted solutions and opportunities that are so clear, appropriate and compelling that they lead him to his visions.

You are the only visionary your life will have. And, like most people, you probably don't look at life as if:

Life is a contest between who you are and who you can be. If you see that as a competition, your life will turn out much better.

To compete, make your vision a good match for your skill set. Aim high, because your skills will grow toward your goals. Act as if you have the power to make it happen and make everything you think and do lead you closer to your vision.

Many of your most common and frequent thoughts actually hold you back. Stated differently, the same thoughts can lead you forcefully toward the future you visualize for yourself.

When you golf, you try to get the ball to go where you have the best opportunity with your next shot. The more accurately you choose your direction, the fewer strokes it will take to get to the hole.

A quarterback doesn't throw the ball to where his receiver is—he throws it to where he wants the receiver to catch the ball.

When you praise a child who is struggling to read, you lead the child toward the outcome you describe in your explanations and encouragement.

> **Your explanations have force. Give them the right direction, and they can lead you to your goals much faster.**

Ingredients of Good Explanations

Make your explanations as accurate as possible.

Give each one a direction that will lead you to be the kind of person you want to be, to have the outcomes you want and to have the kind of life that you want.

View yourself and others in their best possible light.

Lead with encouragement rather than pressure.

Avoid terms like *never, don't, should* and *always*, which exaggerate the facts and the urgency of the matter.

Be careful not to replay your missteps in your mind. Learn from the things you have done wrong, and use what you have learned to improve your future.

The more enthusiastic you are about changing, the easier and faster the changes will come. Make explanations that cause you to reach, and your curiosity and capabilities will deliver as much of what you want as possible.

SERIES A: Topic 7

Shed Anxiety and Boost Creativity in Your Fort

Calming Procedure

Life puts so many pressures on you that it's easy to be tense, irritable, anxious and tired; develop high blood pressure; and make poor decisions. That weakens your confidence and outlook for the future. The standard recommendation is to get a good night's sleep, and to relax in a quiet place for 10 or more minutes a day, breathing slowly and deeply and thinking about the good things in life. When you finish, your outlook will be up and your blood pressure down.

> ***Deciding*** **to be more creative will** ***make*** **you more creative.**

Creative Procedure

Ideas surface easier when you spend time in the conditions in which your brain does its best.

The best place to get fresh ideas and to learn to be creative is in a mental state we'll call your "Fort." If you drag your anxieties into your creative time, you are not as likely to be creative. To be creative, it's best to be at peace and have no agenda. Your Fort is a place where you go to appreciate life and free up your brain. Ideally, it's a physical place that is dark, quiet and peaceful where you really like to be. Or it could be a place you create in your mind. Phones, kids, TV in the background, and other distractions need to be avoided for your session to be as productive as possible. Leave your responsibilities, worries, aggravations, anxieties and negative thoughts at the door.

You will need at least 10 minutes or more to be effective. Since time in your Fort makes all aspects of your life so much more pleasurable and productive, why not go there every day and stay as long as you can? Some people have several Forts and get better ideas on certain subjects in one Fort more than the others.

> **Go to your Fort to get replenished and to spend some quality time with your brain. Turn off the lights, close your eyes, relax and let the calm overtake you. As you unwind, think about your blessings. When you feel content and at peace, let your brain play.**

Never go to your Fort to plead, worry, wish, pray or look for answers or direction. Your brain knows all your relationships, goals and even subjects you have let go of or forgotten. Let your brain pick the topics and the direction it wants to go. It is better to let the ideas happen than to try to make them happen. You are likely to lose creativity if you try to steer it. The more responsibilities you take off your brain, the more processing power it will have to be creative.

Ideas can come and go as fast as the flash of a camera. You are more likely to get pieces of solutions than complete solutions, so write them down before they get away. It becomes an adventure to see where your mind goes. In a single session you might get an idea for an invention, who to call for help, why the meeting with your boss wasn't so good, or where to take your wife for your anniversary.

As you and your brain work as a team, you'll find that you become more creative on a wider range of subjects. In time, you will be able to rely on your creativity to be there when you need it. You will also be able to think as if you are in your Fort without actually *being* in your Fort.

> **You don't need to come up with a single breakthrough idea to make the time you spend in your Fort rewarding. The more you pause to appreciate your life, the better it will be.**

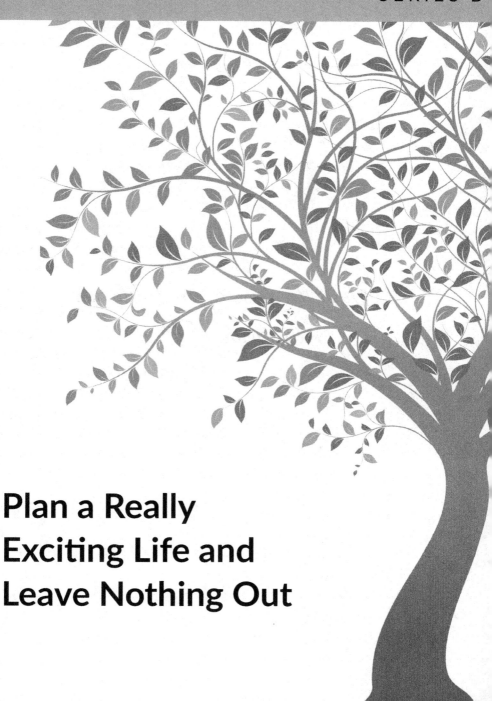

Plan a Really Exciting Life and Leave Nothing Out

Turn the noise of your life into music with a Plan.

SERIES B: Topic 1

Choosing and Using Goals

Many people make the most important decisions of their lives based on their present situation. That's like setting sail for Tahiti in the direction that looks best from the dock! How much planning does the rest of your life deserve? A Harvard study found that, financially, those with a plan did seven times better than those without a plan.

When you write a plan, it becomes the framework for your life. When you haven't written a plan for your future, you are probably using one of these four standard plans:

- You do what seems to work until you feel pain; then you do something else.
- You follow a vague plan, which changes to suit your moods.
- You settle for whatever happens.
- You work so hard at what you are doing at the moment that you don't spend time planning where you want to go.

Your Plan is the map to the life you want. It sets your direction, funnels your energies toward your goals and makes you alert to more facts and ideas that can help you make your Plan happen.

Start your Plan by writing down any thoughts, wishes and imaginings in any order. Then arrange them in the order you will most likely be able to accomplish them. This will create the most efficient path to your goals. The better you plan, the less time you'll waste recovering from unnecessary mistakes and dead ends. Your Plan will align, prioritize and funnel your decisions, energy and resources toward the goals you have chosen. Your Plan will then tell you how you are doing, what's coming up and how to prepare.

To stay on course, you need to be able to look at it often, so you must write it down. Your Plan is your compass.

When you start your Plan, pick as many goals as you want. The best goals will challenge and excite you! Make your goals match your talents.

Start where your Plan will end and plan back toward today.

You can add or remove details and wishes to your Plan as you think of them.

The good news is that the Plan you choose doesn't have to be right; you can change it as your thinking improves.

Big goals don't require giant steps or great talents. You accomplish big goals by doing a good job with the items on your to-do list, and dealing with your goals in the right order.

Goals are not to pressure or force you to try harder. The more interesting your goals are, the more motivation they will give you to go after them.

Your goals are to give you direction, not to put demands on you.

Accomplishing them is not as important as how you live while you are heading toward them.

When you have long-term goals that are clear and exciting, and you are prepared to do whatever it takes to accomplish them, your creativity and motivation make you hyper alert to possibilities and ways to improve your course. Besides, when your plans, priorities and wants are clear, they are easier to follow.

Your life automatically heads toward the life you envision and makes your goals easier to achieve.

ASK YOURSELF

How much quality thought have I put into planning my life?

Which area of my life needs the most planning now?

Which of my goals excites me most?

When I achieve the next big goal, what will I do to celebrate?

SERIES B: Topic 2

Gain Motivation with Visualization

A Plan is like a diary in reverse. It sets out the entries you hope to be able to make during your life. You can have a better future than the one you are headed for, if you can visualize it. So what could be more fun than looking for the right ideas? Here are ways to look for them:

- Travel, read and find ways to learn about anything you are curious about or that inspires you.

- Go to the biggest bookstore in town and pick out the three magazines that interest you most. At least one of those magazines could tell you what you should do to make a living or have a hobby.

- Talk to people who have already done what you'd like to do.

- If you have assumed that your dreams are out of reach, look for ways you could make them happen. Maybe you have overestimated the risk, cost and/or energy required to make them happen. Go to car shows, art shows, garden shows, fairs, concerts, schools, museums, a Sturgis Motorcycle event, the Daytona International Speedway; try hang gliding, parachuting—whatever!

Being able to imagine the life you want makes it easier to obtain.

Nobody is a good planner at first. Begin by writing your wants and wishes for your future as they pop into your head, and then continually improve and rearrange them until your list is full of things you really want and is arranged as well as you can get it. When you choose your goals, assume that your abilities will grow as you progress toward your long-term goals. A good Plan has:

- Goals (what you want and aim for)
- Sequence (the order in which the pieces have to fit together)
- Steps (each action you need to take to get from one goal to the next)
- Tasks (12 or fewer items you will try to get done today or tomorrow, placing at the top the item that will make the most important difference in your life)

Vague Plans produce confused lives.

A well-thought-out Plan doesn't leave out anything important, and it allows for as many exciting details as you can think of. Goals that are in the proper sequence organize your time, money, tools and knowledge so you can move from one goal to the next with as little effort as possible.

> **Your brain is waiting to get you everything you need to succeed. It is guided by your Plan, your opinion of yourself and your images of what your life will be as you progress.**

If you hired a contractor to build your house, you would give him a set of plans and a rendering that shows what the house would look like when finished, right?

Complete and accurate plans reduce the risk of disagreements, and the contractor then moves faster with fewer mistakes.

When you show your friends what your new house will look like, you show them the rendering. The more you love the rendering, the harder you will work to make your house a reality.

Adjust your Plan often so it always represents your best thinking. When you add new goals, make sure they work with your existing goals. Knowing your upcoming goals helps you gather the materials you will need once you actually begin.

> **If your Plan is clear and exciting enough, you will do whatever it takes to make it happen.**

In the next section you will see short- and long-term goal lists.

ASK YOURSELF

Of all the things I did this week, which one produced the most lasting benefits?

Which item for tomorrow will produce the most lasting benefits?

SERIES B: Topic 3

Personal Goals

When you write your personal goals, you describe the type of person you want to be and how you want to live your life. These are more than New Year's resolutions; they set out the qualities you want to have. They are your foundation and remain constant throughout your life.

In the lists that follow, check the boxes next to the goals you want for your life; then add any others you want in the blank lines following the list.

Your Personal Goals

☐ Put God first in my life.

☐ Learn to think better.

☐ Find and use my creativity better.

☐ Improve my judgment.

☐ Control my pride and become less self-involved.

☐ Have a close relationship with every member of my family.

☐ Have a career I love.

☐ Have the best physical, mental and spiritual health I am capable of.

- [ ] Earn enough money to keep my family comfortable and my future secure.

- [ ] Take time to follow my curiosity.

- [ ] Develop friendships.

- [ ] Have time to spend with family and friends.

- [ ] Go on a long vacation far away at least every three years.

- [ ] Create something of lasting value.

- [ ] Own a nice home.

- [ ] Contribute to as many lives as possible.

- [ ] Raise children who will raise good children.

- [ ] Become as valuable a person as possible.

- [ ] Put the right amount of energy into every decision.

- [ ] Have no regrets.

- [ ] Appreciate myself fully.

- [ ] Eat right and exercise to maintain good health.

- [ ] Get along well with everyone.

- [ ] Be reliable.

- [ ] Set a good example for everyone.

- [ ] Shed my emotional baggage, hang-ups, and attitude.

- [ ] Discover and accomplish my purpose in life.

☐ Do as much good as I can.

☐ Have as much fun as I can.

☐ Try to make my attitude of appreciation contagious.

☐ Use all of my potential.

☐ Have a lot of close friends.

☐ Help all of my grandchildren.

☐ Be as clever as possible.

☐ Be generous.

☐ Do a lot of good.

☐ Be an inspiration.

☐ Share my experiences and values with others—especially my family.

☐ Become financially self-sufficient.

☐ Know my purpose and work at it diligently.

Add your own personal goals below:

_____

_____

_____

_____

_____

_____

_____

_____

_____

_____

_____

_____

_____

*The greatest danger is not that our aim is too high
and we miss our goals, but that we aim too low and
reach them.*

—MICHELANGELO

ASK YOURSELF

Which of my goals will produce the most
self-satisfaction?

What is my most pressing relationship goal?

What goal will help me get new friends who are
genuine and more like the person I want to become?

SERIES B: Topic 4

Long-Term Goals

Your personal goals and long-term goals provide the foundation and leadership for your life. They create a funnel that gathers and consolidates all your thoughts, energies and emotions and directs them toward the other goals you have chosen and the life you envision.

A strong plan for life gives you self-assurance and allows you to be happy when the world seems out of control. It prepares you to overcome your immediate problems, and that helps you overcome your biggest problems.

Long-term thinking keeps you adding to your reservoir of knowledge, experience and capabilities. It helps you secure your future and improve your options.

Look at all of your goals as a staircase. Your major goals are landings. Each landing requires you to take a group of steps. To get from one step to the next, you must complete a series of tasks. If you can get your goals, steps and tasks in the right sequence, you will be ready for each as you approach it.

If you can make each stair step the right size, you will be able to climb it without too much effort. Big steps need to be broken into little ones. When you do this, every step you complete builds your self-esteem, gives you an opportunity to celebrate your progress and grants you the ability to see how to prepare to take your next step.

The lists on the following pages set out some of the most popular ideas about how to get to where you want to be at each point in your life.

> **Check the goals you want, and in the blank lines provided below them, write any other goals you desire that would make your life special.**

The lists are only suggestions; personalize your goals and make them fun rather than dutiful.

Make it a priority to pass along your values, knowledge, discipline and experience. If you fail to do so, the monetary assets you pass along won't last long.

Your longest term goals are your End of Life Goals. They set out the conditions you want in place when and after you die.

Choose Heaven

The concept of a God has always been so natural and helpful that even where no models existed, man created religions. Believing in a power greater than our "self" is a key component of most successful rehabilitation programs. It has been a key element in the lives of most people who have recovered from the depths of human existence.

Like a North Star for mariners, heaven can be an unwavering point of light to shoot for.

Having a God who watches out for us is like having a best friend with a GPS that can tell us where we are, route us around hazards and temptations and steer us home. This friend is free for the asking and highly recommended.

End-of-Life Goals

Check or write what you want most for your life in each of the following timeframes.

☐ For God to feel generously thanked by my existence.

☐ To leave my immediate family well loved, educated, taken care of, and well prepared to face the world.

☐ To have helped all those I could.

☐ To have been more of a giver than a taker.

☐ To be debt free and have my life in order.

Goals for Retirement

Financial, personal, giving, relationships, health:

☐ Be close to everyone in my family.

☐ Have no uncomfortable issues with any of my friends or family.

☐ Become smart about investing my money.

☐ Have profitable investments.

☐ Have a yard to landscape.

☐ Own a state-of-the-art sound system.

☐ Own a muscle or a collectible car.

☐   Go to a Super Bowl or World Series game.

☐   Visit Europe and all the states I haven't already seen.

☐   Move to a condo (with no yardwork) on a golf course.

☐   Know a lot about something important.

☐   Put my kids through trade school/college.

☐   Help as many others as I can.

☐   Take up golf, fishing or another sport.

☐   Buy or start a business.

☐   Own some good art.

☐   Write a book.

☐   Own a Harley-Davidson, motor home, or other dream toy.

☐   Pay off my house.

☐   Help get my grandkids through college.

Add your own personal goals below:

_____

_____

_____

_____

_____

_____

_____

_____

_____

_____

_____

_____

_____

_____

_____

ASK YOURSELF

What would I like my descendants to know, think, have and remember about our ancestors?

How prepared is my family to deal with life in my absence?

SERIES B: Topic 5

Intermediate Goals

One-Year Goals

☐ Make better explanations for what I see, experience and anticipate.

☐ Find friends who are more stimulating.

☐ Spend more quality time with my spouse and family.

☐ Make time to "smell the flowers."

☐ Contribute to the community.

☐ Pay off all credit card debt.

☐ Have 6 months' pay saved for an emergency fund.

☐ Live close to work.

☐ Save for tuition.

☐ Become proficient on the computer.

☐ Use my Fort for enjoyment and creativity (see Topic A-7 at GetLifeRight.com).

Add your own personal goals below:

_____

_____

_____

_____

_____

_____

_____

_____

Two- to Five-Year Goals

☐ Get a job where I can learn the most.

☐ Make myself more valuable at work.

☐ Find friends who offer the skills I lack.

☐ Find friends who need the skills I have.

☐ Save money to buy a home.

☐ Buy a reliable car.

☐ Have friends who urge me to be all that I can be.

☐ Visit five nearby states.

☐ Improve my job skills.

☐ Take all job-related courses.

☐ Buy my first house.

☐ Stay in shape.

☐ Obtain a college degree.

☐ Get a job with more potential.

Add your own personal goals below:

_____

_____

_____

_____

_____

_____

_____

_____

_____

_____

_____

Mid-Career Goals

☐ Spend time regularly with my family.

☐ Have a job where I am liked, learning and making a good contribution.

☐ Use my creativity daily.

☐ Own a nice home.

☐ Teach others.

☐ Start a hobby I can share with others.

☐ Spend one-on-one time with each of my kids.

☐ Live close to my job.

☐ Visit new cities.

☐ Own two reliable cars.

☐ Take good trade classes.

☐ Buy a bigger house.

☐ Perform better at work.

☐ Be active at a health club.

☐ Begin my investment program.

☐ Find a better job or start a business.

☐ Save for my kids' college tuition.

☐ Start investing or buy a second home for rental income or appreciation value.

☐   Save for my daughter's wedding.

☐   Take classes on business ownership.

Add your own personal goals below:

_____

_____

_____

_____

_____

_____

_____

_____

_____

_____

_____

_____

SERIES B: Topic 6

Bring on the Spice

Life isn't measured by the number of breaths we take,
but by the moments that take our breath away.

—Anonymous

The Plan you have (or don't have) for your life is a forward-looking résumé of the life you hope to live. If you want anyone to look at the album of your life, make sure you have plenty of highlights. They are the good things, fun things and rewards that can refresh you. Looking forward to good times can make the hard or boring parts of your life much easier.

Elements of a Good Story

Highlights—what is exciting, rewarding or meaningful to you? Some examples might include finding your mate, owning a business, surfing in Australia, racing cars, taking trips around the world, learning to pilot a plane or saving someone's life. Determining your goals and putting them in your Plan for life increases the likelihood of their happening.

Giving—the surest way to build your self-esteem is to do things for others. When you can see how you have touched the life of another person, it enriches your own life. Whether you volunteer at your kid's school, help at the food bank, pull weeds for an elderly person, or find a cure for a disease, the more you give, the more you get.

Romance—how can you find the right person to love? How can you develop the qualities that would attract the type of mate you are hoping to find? In which ways could you make life more fulfilling for your life partner?

Clues—some people have figured out how to buy cars below dealer cost because they followed the clues. There are clues to every mystery. Look for them, and goals you once thought were out of your reach can become attainable.

Adventure—it comes from experiencing situations that are unfamiliar, exciting and daring. Do you want to travel to foreign lands? Would your adventures be challenging physically or mentally? Can you see yourself trying to scuba-dive, skydive or bungee-jump?

The Unknown—what kind of mysterious people, places or events would you like to encounter? Which pastime would you find the most fascinating?

Challenges—boring goals inspire weak effort. Will your objectives be difficult, demanding, or complicated enough to make you feel fulfilled when you achieve them? Which challenge would allow you to use your capabilities in a way that would be the most satisfying to you?

Characters—who do you already know who is interesting, and how can you get to know that person better? How can you attract remarkable friends? Where would you find these people, and how can you keep them in your life? Who would you most like to interview or spend a half day with? There could be hundreds of such people.

Learning—you can plan more adventure into your life when you know more about the world. How should you prepare? What is most important for you to know in order to accomplish your major goals?

Morality—will the message your life gives to the world leave it a better place? How can you begin to build a reputation for being a person of principle?

Intrigue—do you have unexpected obstacles to overcome in order to open up the possibilities for your life? Are there any mysteries you could solve for yourself or your family?

Villains—is there a person or a group standing in the way of something you want? How can you use your charm and imagination to win them over or work around them? Or how can you keep them from impacting your life?

Places—where would you like to live during the various parts of your life? What would you like to experience while you are there?

Also try goals for getting closer to God, having fun family vacations, getting healthy or fit, etc.

Write Your Ideas Down Quickly, Before They Get Away!

SERIES B: Topic 7

The Engine of Your Future

A life that is as good as you can get it requires you to choose your priorities, judge the likely outcome of your choices, and:

Always work on the next most important thing.

In the tiny space between your history and your future is what you do next; that's the only thing you control. That's where the rubber meets the road.

Your Task List Is the Engine of Your Future

If you have chosen your goals and listed the steps you need to accomplish them in the right order, you have created the most efficient path to the life you want. Reaching your goals is now just a matter of doing a good job with the next things on your task list.

When your Plan covers your entire life, it's easier to see the consequences of your everyday choices.

What you choose early in life can prevent you from having more important things later, or throughout your life. When you are lonesome and you buy a puppy to keep you company, you will have bills you didn't expect. You may not be able to find an apartment that will allow pets close to your job or school. You may have to miss a vacation for lack of a pet sitter. You may have to pass on the sales job that requires you to travel. Your pet will consume time you could be investing in your security and career or your social life.

Be careful not to choose a long-term solution for a short-term problem.

Merely writing a Plan will give your self-image a boost, but making progress on your Plan is the best source of motivation and self-esteem. You know you have a good Plan when you are willing to do whatever it takes to make your Plan happen.

Which task should be done first?

- Deal with anything that could become a threat to you.
- Do the tasks that will improve your life the most, and allocate as much time to them as possible.
- Do the tasks you can finalize quickly.
- Do the tasks you can progress on the quickest.
- Put the steps you need to take on your five most important goals on your task list.

Having too many tasks on your list will reduce your effectiveness, so limit your tasks to the number you can keep track of (usually 12 or less). You don't need a task for every area of your life, but don't overlook any area of your life for long.

Write Tasks Like Appointments

Add as much detail as possible to the task list on the next page. Note how the three examples below get progressively easier to follow:

1. "Get teeth fixed"
2. "Call Dr. Wright for an appointment"
3. "Deliver x-rays to Dr. Wright 9 AM for ½ hour 555-8732"

Date	Sample Task List
Today	Ask myself two new questions
Tomorrow	Apply for work at three new places
Mon	Make up with Sally at work
Tues	File application for trade school
Wed	Find better apartment closer to my job
Oct 5	Deliver x-rays to Dr. Wright 9 AM 555-8732

Date	Task List: Not too many, and in order of importance.
	1
	2
	3
	4
	5
	6
	7
	8
	9
	10
	Trip List: The stops you need to make on your next outing.
	Idea List: Write your ideas here before they get away.

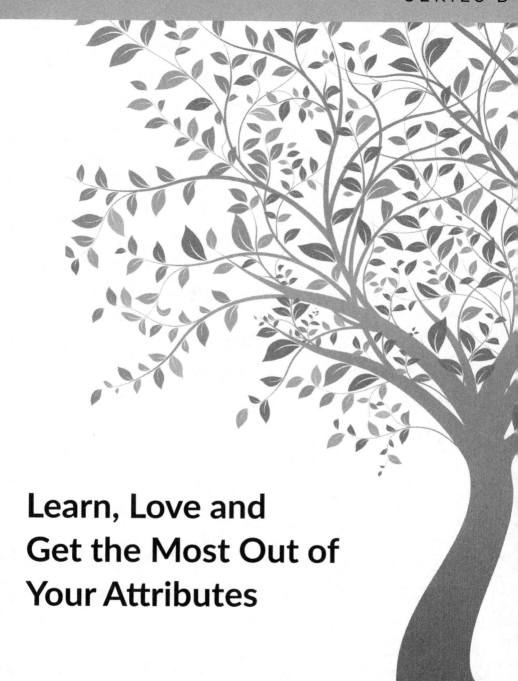

Learn, Love and Get the Most Out of Your Attributes

Leave none of your gifts unopened.

SERIES C: Topic 1

The Way You Are

When you can't seem to make progress, you may undervalue what you can do. You may be unable to find a place where your capabilities can grow and shine. Your life experiences or your assumptions about the world could seem so difficult that a solution is unlikely or too far off. Or you may have nobody to build you up or keep you from being torn down. These are some of the conditions in which you have to become your own mentor.

Your first job as your mentor is to discover and love all aspects of yourself (including your deficits and missteps). You learn to love yourself "the way you are." It doesn't mean accepting everything about you, but you do know that:

- Your capabilities will reveal themselves if you strive.
- You will be able to make good decisions.
- You will do your best in every situation.
- You will be aware of, and adjust to, the impact you have on others.
- You will learn from your mistakes.
- You will enjoy the process.
- What's going right for you will soon get your mind off of those things that had been going wrong.

**Some of your limitations or difficulties that
are beyond your control now can be fixed or
minimized.**

Look at these quotes from *Change Your Brain Change Your Life* by
Dr. Daniel G. Amen, M.D. (ISBN 98-0-8129-2998-0):

> *The actual physical patterns of the brain have a
> dramatic impact on how we think, feel, and behave
> from moment to moment.... We are far too quick to
> attribute people's actions to bad character when the
> source of their actions may not be their choice at all,
> but a problem with brain physiology.... You are not
> stuck with the brain you were born with.... Anxiety,
> depression, anger, obsessiveness, or impulsiveness
> [such as ADD] could be related to how specific struc-
> tures in your brain work.*

> *By looking at the shape and level of activity in the
> structure related to your thinking difficulty, Doctor
> Amen's brain prescriptions can help heal your brain
> and change your life.*

Many people don't know their own best qualities; so they tend to
undervalue themselves.

**It's easy to assume that others get through life
more easily than you do, but everyone struggles in
his own way.**

All winners start as beginners. Once you are willing to look like
a beginner, you can learn much more quickly. One reason young
kids pick up languages more quickly than adults is that they
haven't learned to be concerned about what others might think
if they goof.

A baby learning to walk may have a droopy diaper as she stumbles around, pulls objects off the table, bumps her head on the furniture, and spills everything within reach. Yet her parents view all these missteps as progress rather than failure. Face it: In the scheme of life, even the smartest and most accomplished among us are still just stumbling our way into our future.

In impoverished countries, kids earn money or work early in life because the survival of their family depends on it. As a result, those kids have high self-esteem. If your self-worth comes from having the best toys instead of from using your best efforts, then your self-esteem is only as valuable as your toys.

> **Keep your life in balance and perspective by striving to make the best contribution to the world that you can.**

Possessions and power are demanding; they complicate your life and keep you from appreciating what you have. If you were ill, near death, or in prison, you wouldn't be asking for luxuries; what you'd want is to be able to feel the warmth of the sun on your skin, take a walk in the park, or get a hug from a loved one.

There is an old folktale about a woman who lived in medieval times. Every day she carried water from the river to the home where she worked as a servant. One of the two pots she used had a crack in it. One day the cracked pot told the lady how ashamed it was that it was always half empty by the time it got back home. The lady told the pot that she had planted seeds along the trail and the water that spilled made them grow. Those flowers were the source of her greatest joy. Suddenly the cracked pot changed from feeling useless to being proud.

You can go from being unhappy to being happy just as quickly. All you have to do is appreciate yourself not only for what you hope to be able to do but for what you are doing today.

You can never reach a point where you have nothing to give.

You make contributions with your weaknesses as well as with your gifts. You can be thankful for the beggar, who probably never had a day of peace or security in her life, who lay dying in a gutter in Calcutta, India. Her moaning was heard by a young nun who held her as her life slipped away. That was the moment Mother Teresa made the decision to dedicate her life to helping the "poorest of the poor."

A boy who was born with no immune system grew up in a small germ-proof enclosure. His positive, friendly personality charmed everyone until his death at age 14. His caregivers told people that "he was touched by no one, but he touched everyone." If his life were measured by his financial impact, he would be considered a loss to society. The fact that people are still inspired by him today is proof that he enriched the world.

Plants make several kinds of seeds to ensure their survival. Soft seeds become compost quickly, ordinary seeds grow into new plants, but a few seeds are so hard that they won't germinate. They may lay idle for years before being eaten by birds. Luckily, birds have trouble digesting them, but their stomach acids weaken the seeds, and when those seeds are passed they are finally able to take root and grow. In the middle of a forest that has burned or that has died because of blight, new growth begins from hard seeds dropped by birds. Your life may have been hard, you may have gone through some caustic stuff, and you may have passed through some tight spots, but you are exactly what the world needs. You are essential the way you are.

Wishing you were more than you are can make you less than you are.

You are most valuable to a team when you play the position for which you are best suited. Striving to fill a position you can't quite master will not make either you or anyone else happier.

You can see all of mankind averaged into 100 people in *Who Lives in the Global Village?* by Donella H. Meadows (http://www. empowermentresources.com/info2/theglobal village.html). It is paraphrased as follows.

---

57 would be Asians, 21 would be Europeans, 14 would be Americans (all three continents), and 8 would be Africans.

52 would be women and 48 would be men.	6 people in the USA would possess 50% of all the wealth on earth.
30 would be Caucasians.	1 would have a university degree.
30 would be Christians.	1 would own a computer.
86 would be heterosexual.	70 would be illiterate.
2 billion people would be unable to read.	1 would be dying and 1 would be being born.
80 would live in poverty.	50 would suffer from malnutrition.

You Are Blessed;
What Will You Do with Your Gifts?

ASK YOURSELF

How would I act on this matter if I had more confidence?

Which of my skills have I undervalued?

SERIES C: Topic 2

Learning Made Easier

Take comfort in these words from Travis Bradberry and Jean Greaves, authors of *Emotional Intelligence 2.0:*

People with the highest levels of intelligence (IQ) outperform those with average IQs just 20 percent of the time, while those with average IQs outperform those with high IQs 70% of the time.

Proper and stable emotions are more essential to your success than your intelligence. Your desire, energy, drive, resilience, coping skills and social skills, along with your ability to stick to a plan, are better predictors of your potential than your intelligence. With the right motivation and common sense, you can learn or acquire almost any skill you lack.

More often than not, slow learners think of learning as difficult and potentially embarrassing, so they avoid it. Some won't even try to learn information that is essential to their progress and well within their ability to master.

Learning may seem hard, but nothing is as hard as trying to get through life without learning.

Thinking you can't learn is more likely to keep you from learning than the lack of any skills. People with below-average intelligence can be very imaginative, just as extremely intelligent people can lack creativity and common sense. Comparing your abilities to those of others or blaming your learning problems on yourself or someone else will do nothing but reduce your ability to think.

Learning Problems

Personal—self-image, anxiety, confusion, anger, self-pity, peer pressure and fear of failure.

Physical—hearing or vision problems, Dyslexia, Autism and memory limitations.

Place—background noise, clutter, poor lighting or any other kind of distraction, plus the lack of a proper place to learn.

Reading and learning skills develop slowly; you have to be patient. Pressuring yourself often slows down the process by making work out of it. Everyone learns differently. Some people learn best by reading, others by seeing, others by demonstrations, and others by doing.

Nothing helps you to learn more than succeeding.

The slower you read, the more selective you need to be about what you read. Concentrate on the subjects that will improve your life or that you are passionate about. A slow reader can become an avid reader if he is excited enough about the subject.

You probably know someone who thinks of himself as a slow learner, yet he can pick up a video game and play almost nonstop until he masters it. When he eventually stops, it's usually because he stopped learning. He wasn't really a slow learner; he just hadn't been motivated to learn the things that had been put in front of him. Kids who do poorly on assigned material often do very well on subjects they have chosen. Likewise, they do much better when they can see how the material they are studying will benefit their lives.

About 15% of us have significant learning problems, which include conditions such as attention deficit disorder, hyperactivity (ADD or ADHD), dyslexia and autism. The thought processes of some children with autism have been described as thinking in pictures. Pictures containing multiple subjects are hard to file, so many fall into a box, like puzzle pieces. When the child wants to make a new thought out of them, he has trouble finding them and has to piece them together to complete his thoughts. It takes him longer to produce thoughts, and he has to be creative to do so. Those who are able to do so often become very imaginative, especially in the creative fields.

> **Your ability to think isn't as important as your ability to know what to think about.**

Like everyone else, you have limits on the amount and types of information you can recall, process or hold in your mind while you are forming new thoughts or making decisions.

Most of the time, your judgments, thoughts and decisions can be just as good as those of people who can take in and process much more information than you can. The key is to limit your attention to the subjects that are most important to you.

Phil was confident he could put just about anything together without reading the instructions—that is, until he had a smart phone. It worked in ways that were unexpected. Whenever he saw a stranger with a similar phone, he'd ask for a tip on how to use it. After three months, he had learned only about 5% of what his new phone had to offer. Like that phone,

> **You have capabilities beyond your wildest
> imaginings. If you don't read your instructions, you
> will under-utilize the capabilities you're aware of,
> and fail to use those you aren't.**

Nobody can make you learn if you assume you can't or don't want to; but if you do want to, nobody can stop you.

Many people become learning-resistant as children and continue to assume they will have reading difficulties as adults. All they need to change that belief is one book that holds their attention from beginning to end. Once they see how much smarter they can become by reading, the excuses they once used for not reading will make them blush.

If you are dissatisfied with your brain power, imagine yourself on a cruise ship. You are looking through a porthole, and another person is looking from the deck. By moving from side to side and up and down, you can see almost everything the person on deck can see. If you are focused on the most important part of the scene, you may be less distracted by things in the bigger picture that are not as important.

You can compete favorably with people who can take in more information at a time than you can, if the things you focus on (and think about) are the right ones for you. For example, your cruise can be very satisfying whether you are looking through a porthole or from the deck.

> **You limit your potential when you judge your
> future ability by your first attempts, or when you
> don't stick with a goal long enough.**

It might take an hour to assemble a toy the first time, 40 minutes the second time, 20 the third time, and less time for each of the next 10 tries.

Concentrate on learning subjects that come naturally to you, instead of subjects that are hard for you. When you need to know a difficult subject, get as familiar with it as you can; then hire a tutor or the best consultant you can find and afford.

Gain as much specialized knowledge as possible in the subjects you like and do well in. When employees are getting laid off, people who have specialized knowledge are usually the last ones to go.

During World War II, men who struggled in school often joined the army. When they got out of the service their motivation and maturity helped most of them outperform students who were transferring into college from high school. Their abilities hadn't changed, but their desire to learn had.

World-famous pianist Arthur Rubinstein played beautifully until he was 89, long after most people's memory, vision and finger skills are gone. He learned to work around the limitations by selecting songs he knew well and practicing them until he could play them without thinking.

If you still have trouble learning, it's okay. You don't need a good memory or to be good at school to be highly successful. You can learn what you like. A mason from Mexico learned only 30 words of English in 20 years. But he could design, frame, and pour cement, and he could lead a crew of skilled workers to create complicated and exquisite patios. Let your interests lead you to what you can do best. The success you get from that will help you work around your weaknesses.

A small brain working on important things will accomplish more than a big brain working on things that aren't.

ASK YOURSELF

What do I do best right now?

What would I most like to become good at?

Who can teach me?

How soon can I start?

What have I assumed I can't do that I should try again with persistence and an open mind?

SERIES C: Topic 3

Use All of Your Brain Power

If you feel your life is a mess, what you are actually feeling is your disappointment with the way you have been thinking. When you project those thinking skills into the future, your future shrinks because your confidence shrinks.

Ways You May Be Underestimating Your Thinking Ability

1. You presume those who are progressing faster than you are more intelligent. People with the same amount of intelligence that you have can appear much smarter when they have learned to use their intelligence better than you have learned to use yours. You are probably much smarter than you realize.

2. Your classmates always seemed smarter than you. However, you may have been a year younger than they, depending on your birth date.

3. Your gifts could be in subjects like art, trades, business or sports, that aren't taught at regular schools.

4. You haven't worked with enough people or situations to know how capable you are.

5. Your parents may not have been able to give you the

encouragement, motivation or help you needed. Perhaps they never got it from their parents.

6. The atmosphere or study conditions at home may have made it difficult for you to do your homework.

7. You could have had a series of bad teachers or been in classes where your teachers couldn't keep order.

8. Your appearance, manner or misbehavior could have discouraged others from helping you.

9. You could have moved through school with a wave of exceptionally gifted classmates, or exceptionally poor students, either of which might have put you behind your peers.

10. You may never have seen any long-term value in what you were being asked to learn.

11. You are so anxious or impatient that your brain jumps around and keeps you from listening or concentrating. You can't remember what you don't hear.

12. You assume intelligence is more important than it really is. In most cases, though, common sense, motivation, imagination, courage, hard work and determination are more essential to success than raw brainpower.

13. You have falsely assumed you aren't good at thinking and have quit trying, instead of demanding better explanations and decisions of yourself.

14. On a few occasions, anxiety, distractions or emotional issues cause you to bring up facts that aren't quite right. Using the wrong name for a person you don't know very well might

have embarrassed you in front of others. Your fear of making more mistakes causes your brain to worry about remembering while you are *trying* to remember, which reduces your *ability* to remember.

15. Your expectations for yourself cause you to think in anxiety instead of peace.

16. When you have difficulty trying to work while someone is waiting or trying to talk to you, it may have nothing to do with your ability to reason. Many people are just not able to do more than one thing at a time.

17. You have the correct thoughts but they don't all come when you need them. On any subject of importance, write down your thoughts as they come to you. When you think you have enough of the right thoughts, pull out the file and write your conclusion. The process of sorting and prioritizing your ideas will draw out more ideas.

18. Your anxieties have made it difficult to concentrate. Being behind makes them worse. Find ways to get them settled down and your ability to learn will increase. Start by loving yourself more as you are.

Ways to Improve Your Thinking

1. Reduce the number of subjects your brain has to think about.

2. Improve the quality of things you let your brain work on.

3. Allow yourself more time to come up with answers.

4. Presume you have more capabilities than you can discover in your entire lifetime, and it's your job (and pleasure) to develop as many capabilities as you can.

5. Use your empathy for yourself and others to understand what effect your emotions are having on your decisions.

6. Be quicker to try the thinking of others.

7. Think of finding the information you need as a riddle rather than a chore.

8. When all the alternatives are unsatisfactory, get fresh ideas in your Fort (see Topic A-7 at GetLifeRight.com). Make the subject the last thing you think about before you go to sleep.

Accomplishing something important can be just a thought away.

Alexandra was only four years old and she had been fighting cancer most of her life. Her thought was to operate a lemonade stand to raise money for other kids who had cancer. In her first year she raised $2,000. By the time she passed away at age eight, she had raised $1 million. People are still opening Alex's Lemonade Stands. By 2012 she had raised over $50 million for children with cancer.

ASK YOURSELF

Where is the best place for my Fort?

Achieving what task will give me the most momentum?

What's the most desirable reward I can create for finishing the difficult task ahead of me?

SERIES C: Topic 4

Use All of Your Creativity

Behind every thought, explanation and invention is a better one, but you will never find it if you aren't looking for it. Cleverness is applied creativity. It's a state of mind that is active, playful and curious, and it's always looking for a better way. There's good news for those who think they aren't creative.

Your ideas don't have to come from within you.
They are everywhere, they are free, and they're
hoping to be found.

Like a tuning fork can repeat the vibrations it was created to receive, the subjects that interest you are the ones you have been created to receive. The number and quality of ideas you get depends on how open and curious you are, how carefully your antenna is focused on the subject and how important the subject is to you.

Ideas come in bits and pieces. If you store them close to each other, turn them over in your mind and look for relationships between the parts, you begin to see how they can be made to fit into new thoughts and solutions.

Learning how to become clever makes you alert to more possibilities. You can accomplish more with your brain than with your brawn. You don't have to be brilliant or to work harder than everyone else to accomplish great feats, if you develop your ability to think.

You can compete with people who have more intelligence by making better use of the intelligence you have.

You feel clever when you use your common sense to win, to make a point or to make a contribution that is out of the ordinary. Cleverness means thinking with agility, energy and a sense of humor. It comes from being able to see through your own prejudices to find details others have missed.

You have "constant" cleverness that operates as if it's an invisible propeller attached to your forehead that cannot be turned off. It is imaginative and forceful at driving you in the direction you are going, wherever that is, good or bad.

You have "imaginative" cleverness. It is trainable. It starts when you decide to use it, and it grows with use and exposure to new and exciting information and change.

With every new subject write down your objective and every option you can think of. Then put the paper down and get your mind off of the subject for a while. When you come back, you will have even more ideas and new ways of looking at what you've already written. Repeat this process until you love your idea or plan of action.

Use your thinking power to find answers rather than to reexamine the problem. Dedicate less than 10% of your thinking on the problem and more than 90% on the solution.

Some successes come from single big ideas, but most come from a steady stream of small ideas or the use of a clever process.

The best way to accomplish a big project is to work on the part that is easiest or most familiar to you. Once you are comfortable with it, work on the next easiest part. As you gain experience, the parts ahead of you will become more familiar and therefore easier.

Once you get a job where you can use your cleverness, you will never want a routine job. The more cleverness you use, the more you can count on it in the future. When you know you can rely on your cleverness, you will attempt larger challenges.

If you need to earn 3% more money, you may be able to work hard enough to earn that amount at your present job. If you want to double your pay, you will need a job that motivates you. You may have to create a job yourself. It may require more training, a product to market, or a business to start, but all those tasks would be more fun than just working harder at what you are already doing.

Like exercise, the more often and more completely you use your creativity, the more you can rely on its being there when you need it.

You can't know all you are capable of because, like the horizon, as you approach what you'd expect to be your limit, it expands ahead of you.

ASK YOURSELF

How can I use my cleverness to make a living doing something I love?

What issue or relationship needs my cleverness now?

SERIES C: Topic 5

Emotions That Work

The first step in mastering your emotions is to become more aware of them and their effect on other people.

Every emotion you use has a purpose and a consequence you are responsible for.

Tips for Becoming a Better Observer of Your Emotions

- High and low mood swings make you unpredictable. They make others cautious around you, and they make it harder for you to stay focused.

- Anxiety, fear and uncertainty make it harder for you to try new things, so these feelings rob you of experiences that could enrich your life.

- "Baggage" (the residue of bad self-talk) can drive away the friendships you need.

- Anger, hatred, bitterness, jealousy and resentment close your mind and cause you to talk and act in such ways that others will consider you toxic and attempt to avoid you.

- Insecurity makes you unable to trust yourself and makes you dependent on the approval of others.

- If you assume the emotions of others are honest and not intended to manipulate you, you will be more patient with them, and they will be more accepting of you.

- You have been doing what you have been doing because you thought it was working. Has it worked? What would work better?

Your reaction to a problem can damage a relationship more than the problem itself. For example, suppose your wife volunteers to get you some parts at the store. She brings you the parts that match your request, but they aren't exactly what you wanted. Since they are on sale, the items she bought can't be returned. Your anger can be far worse than the lost money or having to take a second trip to the store.

Background Thoughts for Healthier Emotions

1. The one assigning blame to everyone else is often the one causing the problem; and that individual could be you.

2. The person who is the loudest is trying to intimidate, often because he can't or doesn't want to explain his position.

3. Would you want others to see the way you are being if they were people you really respected?

4. The people you are dealing with may not be reasonable.

5. Is this fight worth winning? What will I gain if I win?

6. Participants in an argument will naturally be defensive. If you acknowledge their good points, it will make them more open to your points.

7. To help you make responses that fit the situation better, always look beyond the behavior you are observing. It could be caused by a deeper problem in another part of the other person's life.

8. If you always react in a way that is unflattering to you, you give others the power to make you look bad merely by provoking you. Some will do it for sport.

9. Your own judgments and longings to fix others can be what is causing you pain.

10. It is safest and usually right to assume that when you are having a problem with another person, he or she will be aware of it.

11. When you can accept others as they are, the reasons for heightened emotions go away.

12. The way you react to a situation is what causes you pain, not the situation itself.

13. When confronted with something that causes your emotions to flare up, pause to collect your thoughts and get better information before reacting.

14. Your expectations on one issue can make you anxious on all others; more realistic expectations can lower your level of agitation.

If the emotions you have been using aren't working, change them. Ask the victims of your emotions how you can change, but know that you won't get this information unless you can convince them that it will be safe to tell you and that you truly want to change.

When you unload or overreact, your ego is giving you permission to disrespect and discount the other people involved.

Avoid situations that might trigger emotional outbursts. If something has to be dealt with, allow yourself to calm down and get your thoughts together. Don't feel like you have to react immediately.

The emotions you use, you choose.

Two children died early as teenagers. Their dad chose to be bitter and made everyone around him miserable for the next 10 years. When he finally admitted that being angry wasn't working, he let it go. When he changed his explanation to "God loaned me those kids; I was blessed to have them while I did," he rebuilt his relationship with his family and friends, and his business picked up dramatically.

ASK YOURSELF

Which of my emotions are holding me back?

How would others describe the way I act when I am under pressure or confronted with an unexpected difficulty?

How can I become easier to be around?

SERIES C: Topic 6

Confidence and Self-Esteem

The experiences of your life are passing in front of you as if on a conveyor belt. How you respond to each experience will either increase or decrease your potential and affect the quality of things that show up on your conveyor belt in the future. When you know you can handle just about anything that comes down that conveyor, you have confidence.

If only two experiences pass in front of you in a week, you have very little opportunity to develop your confidence. If your conveyor belt is full of items and moving fast, you may initially strain to keep up, but soon you will learn to make decisions quickly.

Before you get too proud of how much you can accomplish with your conveyor, be aware there are other conveyor belts in the world. Many of them have better experiences on them than the one in front of you. A nice amount of work at the right belt might produce a far better life for you than working with all your might on the one in front of you. Never stop looking for ways to get the right opportunities to pass in front of you.

> *"Confidence is knowing that when you make up your mind to do something you will do whatever it takes to make it happen. You will succeed even though you*

know that there will be difficulties, you will be fearful at times, others will see you struggling, and you will have some setbacks."

—Barbara De Angelis

Your confidence increases when:

- You take charge of your own life.
- You stay focused and try as hard as you can.
- You take advantage of the information available to make better decisions.
- You are making progress.
- You feel comfortable asking for help.
- You control your emotions.

Your confidence decreases when:

- You procrastinate or wait for something outside of yourself to happen before you begin.
- You require yourself to win instead of accepting your best effort.
- You are afraid to take risks.
- You aren't realistic about what you can do.
- You fear the unknown.
- You wait for others to make your decisions for you.
- You choose goals that are not well suited to your set of skills.
- You can't visualize how life will be if you actually do succeed.

If a task can't be accomplished well, a confident person won't dwell on what went wrong; he will capture the lessons learned and use them in the future.

Confidence is a very important part of your self-esteem, but your self-esteem is a lot more complicated. It is a measure of your character and the quality of your spirit. It reflects how well you think you are doing with your personal goals (see Topic B-3 at GetLifeRight.com) and the things you value most.

Self-esteem reflects how proud you are of yourself, the choices you have made, and your ability to make good choices in the future. It is knowing your successes won't inflate your self-image and rejection won't crush it.

No success is everlasting, and no defeat is ever final.

A decision that's made for the right reasons and turns out wrong might shake your confidence but not your self-esteem. Self-esteem deals with your integrity—how satisfied you are that you have done your best and gathered the right amount of information for your decisions. It grows when you have a good plan for life that is working. Self-esteem is hard to find when you don't know where you are going, or don't like the direction of your life.

A condition that may cause your self-esteem to suffer in one part of your life can help you in another. Hector couldn't afford a uniform or get to practice, so he never got to play sports with the kids in the neighborhood. There was a shop near his house where they customized cars. The workmen let him hang out there, for which he kept the place clean and fetched tools. By the time his classmates got out of Little League, he already knew how to fix many things on cars. By the time he got out of high school he had his own custom car and looking forward to having his own shop.

What you think is the outer limit of your capability can often be a small fraction of it. You can accomplish more than you can imagine if you get help developing your gifts and get them positioned for the right opportunities.

In every interaction where a problem arises between people there are those who have nothing to offer, take sides or don't want to get involved, but there are some who make important contributions. Those people might console, empathize, listen, mediate or help in any way, but what he or she is also doing is leading. They steering the emotions and the search for a solution in the direction which is the best for all parties. You may not feel ready to lead now, but if you start supporting the person who is coming closest to leading you will soon become a leader. It is an important role for us all. It's a skill we can all use; especially parents.

Instead of telling yourself that you can't do something, which sounds like a permanent condition, tell yourself that you are unfamiliar with the task. This statement suggests that it is a temporary condition if it was important enough to you, you could do it.

Self-esteem builds over time, but you can start any time by making your next decision a good one.

Your self-esteem increases when:
- You know what is right or wrong.
- You have clear priorities.
- You discover and pursue your purpose for living.

- You are aware of the effect your actions are having on others.
- You are at peace with the people who are important to you.
- You make a decision you are proud of.
- You have a plan for life and it is working

ASK YOURSELF

What goal can I put everything I've got into?

What is my next most important task?

Which part of me am I the most proud of?

What area of my life is lowering my self-esteem?

SERIES C: Topic 7

Acting As If

Everything you do fits into the image you have of yourself. Your self-image is what you have concluded about yourself, and what you believe others think about you. It is a combination of all the ways you think you have to be in order to be you. Each way is a role you can change. If you don't manage your roles well, you can get stuck in roles that don't work and that hold you down. Your self-image reflects how proud you are of the roles you are now playing.

Discover your capabilities by "acting as if" you already have them.

Attempting to change can be challenging, uncomfortable, or even terrifying if you are unsure of yourself or expect to be criticized. Every actor who steps out on stage feels nervous at first. Look at what you are about to do as an attempt and a learning opportunity.

If you don't have a clear idea of how you'd rather be, you can give yourself a vague role and clarify it as you go. Just "act as if," then do more of what works and less of what doesn't. Your new role will become natural to you quite quickly, especially when it feels like who you truly want to be.

The process of "acting as if" doesn't create the capabilities you desire; it reveals the capabilities you already have.

"Acting as if" is the gateway to experience, and experience reinforces your capabilities. The people who seem to be living their lives as you would like to live yours got there by "acting as if" they had capabilities sooner and more often than you did. They made each new role more interesting and challenging than the one before it.

You can put yourself in the role of being wise, charming, fun, self-assured, concerned, friendly, successful, energetic, prudent, even-tempered or skillful. You could choose to be a more capable parent or a more caring spouse. Actually, you don't have to choose between these qualities; you can grow into them all as you go.

When you "act as if" you can do something, you will be faking it a little bit. If you are concerned others will know (which might be embarrassing), compare that to what they will think if they find out you were too timid to try.

The first few times you step into a new role, your brain (like your friends) will try to get you back to your comfortable habits. Initially your change will seem like a halfhearted New Year's resolution. Make sure you assert your new role long enough for your brain and your friends to realize they will have to adjust to your will. This usually doesn't begin until you persist for 10 days. If you are emotionally dependent on a behavior that is holding you back, it can take much longer.

When you are confident the roles you have chosen are the right ones, and they are working for you, you will enjoy life so much that you won't have time to wonder about your self-image or who's looking at you.

ASK YOURSELF

Which of my current roles are slowing my progress?

Which one should I work on first?

How would I improve it?

Of the people I know, who uses the "acting as if" concept the best?

SERIES C: Topic 8

The Power of Wanting

When you fail to make adequate progress, it is usually because you don't know what to want, you think you can't get what you want or you don't know how to get in a position to do what interests you. If you want something badly, those doubts won't be enough to hold you back.

> **Having a goal you are passionate about gives you courage, helps you harness your creativity and energy, and makes you more aware of new possibilities.**

Your self-esteem takes a hit when you have to do something that doesn't interest you. When a project interests you enough you become unaware of many things that normally bug you, and you are less likely to be distracted. When you love what you are doing, it ceases to be work; that is why it is often easier to go after big goals that you love rather than small ones you don't care about. Trying and failing is a better experience than not pursuing what you want.

> **When you don't ask for enough, you get what you ask for.**

You can seem to be doing well and still be operating below capacity. You end up with less than what you could have had when you:

- Assume you are incapable.
- Are afraid to let others see you learn or fail.
- Are lazy, or they think of effort as hard work.
- Are reluctant to get started.
- Never try very hard.
- Aren't paying attention.
- Are working too hard think or plan.
- Don't trust yourself.
- Can't picture anything good happening to you.
- Set impossible goals.
- Wait for the right time to start.
- Never set goals for the future.
- Believe you have to keep doing what you are doing.
- Won't take responsibility.
- Assume others will judge you harshly.
- Believe life is more difficult than it is (or that the cards are stacked against you).

When you are unwilling to pursue your dreams or even admit them, it's easy to assume your dreams are out of reach or that you are helpless on the matter.

Wanting something and going after it builds your self-confidence, alerts you to possibilities and helps you get moving. It gets you past "*I can't* make this happen" to "*How can* I make this happen?"

- If you spend less time thinking about your problems, you will have more time to think about solutions.
- If you try and fail, you can always try again.
- Others will think more of you if you try and fail, than if

you fail to try; and they always seem to know which of these you are doing.

- You may assume others will appreciate your efforts and give you a hand.
- People are more likely to treat you well if you expect they will.
- It will be easier for people to like you if they think you like them.
- There is a lesson you can learn from every attempt you make.
- Overthinking issues will keep you from getting started. "Analysis leads to paralysis!"

Picture yourself as a man in a race. You are out of energy and heading for the sideline to quit when you notice a woman you like watching you. All of a sudden you have a burning desire to look good, and you sprint to the finish. Turns out you weren't out of energy; you were merely discouraged. When it seems like you can't do something, don't quit. Look for a fresh perspective or new motivation, take a break, and then get back in the race. You will have the power if you are going after something you really want.

A word of caution: Aside from wanting the wrong things, you can damage your life by wanting something too much or for the wrong reasons. When you need to win to feed your ego, it can take away from other parts of your life. If you have attached too much of your self-worth to your goal, failing to achieve it can make you feel like a failure. To ensure that doesn't happen, enjoy and appreciate every day as you live it. Baseball players strike out far more often when they try to hit home runs; just getting on base more often can be more satisfying. Golfers who swing too hard don't hit the ball as far as those with a natural swing. Choosing goals that are natural for you increases your chances of success and reduces your chances of failure.

ASK YOURSELF

Am I going at life as if I want a trophy or a finisher's ribbon?

What am I passionate about?

When I achieve the next big goal, what will I do to celebrate?

SERIES C: Topic 9

Benefit from All
Your Turning Points

A turning point is an event, idea, revelation or realization—good or bad—which is so powerful that it causes you to change the way you proceed with your life.

Negative Turning Points

Events—the death of a loved one, a car accident, an illness, an injury, incarceration, the loss of a friendship, a bad marriage, an unplanned pregnancy or a breach in the relationship between a parent and child.

Decisions—drunk driving, fighting, stealing, cheating, using drugs, reckless behavior, marrying the wrong person, not studying, "hanging" with bad people or having too much debt.

Influences—unhealthy siblings or friends, bullies, bad role models, abusive spouses, critical teachers or unskilled parents.

Good or bad turning points call for thinking through all the ways you can react. Every choice is capable of producing unintended consequences for yourself and others. It takes time to imagine those possibilities.

Turning points can be caused by something as minor as your mistaken understanding of what another person meant. Worse than that, you may have thought you heard someone say something he never said.

Your girlfriend could say "A group of us are going to meet at Shawna's house around 7:30 p.m." Your girlfriend is very popular and you aren't, so you've been expecting her to dump you any time. You thought she said she was going to Sean's house (Sean is a guy), and you know he is a very bad person. You think if she is willing to go to his house she isn't going to keep dating you, so you give up. She doesn't know why you didn't show up, or why you stopped calling her. The rest of your dating life you do poorly because you are convinced you can't hold onto a powerful woman and must be a lousy date. The explanation you created was based on false information which you treated as truth and used to your own detriment.

In another example, a woman separates from her husband and poisons her kids' attitude against him. The kids restructure their lives around the belief that their father abandoned them, never knowing the truth—that she refused mail and packages from him, and then moved them across the country with no forwarding address. If the father finds them and the kids get a chance to hear his side of the story, a few moments with Dad could eliminate a lot of sadness for him and the kids.

Another false explanation that has damaged the lives of many children comes from comments made by other kids. They may tell a child his dad is strict because he hates the child. The boy starts reading the wrong meaning into everything his dad says or does. The son's hurt turns to resentment and then defiance. Feeling isolated, he seeks comfort among misfits who teach him how to get and use drugs and make a mess of his life—all of which he wrongly blames on his dad.

Sometimes, in response to negative turning points, you can hurt yourself while trying to get even with the people who hurt you. Those people can be completely unaware of your suffering. You do this by holding a grudge or by demanding additional attention, sympathy or coddling from others. You put distance between yourself and the people who hurt you; you act as if you can take care of yourself; you try to be perfect, deny your feelings, hide from life or fail to try; or you self-medicate (with drugs, alcohol, food, etc.).

Those considering suicide are usually basing their emotional state on explanations that are completely or mostly false. They then rule out the explanations that don't support their false beliefs. Then they play those thoughts over and over in their mind until there is no room for any alternatives. To get away from the pain they consider suicide—a permanent solution to a temporary problem.

Before you let a turning point change your life, give it a fair hearing:

- Ask all witnesses and those involved what they think happened and how they felt about it.
- Decide not to allow the issue to have power over you.
- Grow past it rather than adjust to it.
- Stop replaying the negative parts of the event in your head.
- Ask friends who are wise, safe and supportive to give you their opinions on the incident as you describe it to

them, especially if they've had a somewhat comparable experience.

- Give up any of your own behaviors that might have exposed you to or contributed to the event.
- Make the way you change produce the best outcome for as many parties to the event as possible.

No Positive Turning Point Found

Rodney Dangerfield (the "I don't get no respect" comedian), by his own admission, was an unhappy man. In interviews he claimed he never got any recognition from his parents, and the scars from his youth followed him into adulthood. Shortly before his death at age 82, Rodney was quoted as saying, "People love my work, but they don't love me," and "Making people laugh didn't make me happy."

It appears as though Rodney never turned the corner. The way he explained his bad experiences to himself played a part in keeping others at a distance. If you were in a situation like his, which of the following explanations would help you most?

Check the box for the three explanations you would find most helpful:

☐ Get your mind off yourself.

☐ Have a purpose you are passionate about.

☐ Appreciate more and complain less.

☐ Forgive your parents.

☐ Let go of the payoff you get from acting like a victim.

☐ Move away from the phonies or "hangers on" to a new place where you can find genuine friends.

- [ ] Make fixing your problem more of a priority.
- [ ] Seek medical treatment for depression.
- [ ] Remind yourself: You are as happy as you decide to be.

ASK YOURSELF

Changing which one of my beliefs would make the biggest difference in my life now?

Which of my current beliefs is holding me back the most?

What part of my life would benefit most from a complete makeover in my thinking?

SERIES C: Topic 10

Shedding Notions of Suicide

Notes on Suicide for Those at Risk

Many completely logical people with great lives ahead of them get caught up in the emotions of the moment and contemplate suicide. While not intended, it is often a control issue and a selfish act. A suicide hurts everyone and leaves them feeling like a hand grenade has gone off in their midst.

Typically, you have assumed the worst possible outcomes on a lot of issues and played them in your head so many times that no fresh ideas or reasonable alternatives can get in. No matter what you have done, or what is happening to you, that can change for the better quickly.

Thousands of people who decided not to take their lives are loving life and being loved by others.

There are thousands of people who live just to help people who are struggling. Your need is not a burden to them; it would make them feel wonderful if they could help you.

To eliminate the logjam of thoughts and emotions in your head, relax; then imagine you were shipwrecked on a deserted island.

Your survival instincts would start solving your immediate problems and shove your previous worries into the background. Fortunately, a change of scenery or people for a while may be all it takes. Do something or go somewhere new or different for you. While you are being refreshed, limit your thoughts to all the things that could go right, and how fortunate you are. Try to go where there will be interesting activities, not to where it is quiet or you will be alone.

Read all of Chapter 2 on "Valuing Yourself." See where you fit into the world. Look at the Global Village near the bottom of Topic C-1 at GetLifeRight.com. Also view the video at http:/www.flixxy. com/wonderful-world-david-attenborough.htm.

Not dealing with your problems allows them time to become more serious. Get help early. Let someone help you, and don't stop looking until you find the help you need. New medications are available that can reduce anxiety and allow your brain to relax so you can start thinking clearly again.

Skills for Helping Those at Risk

If there is a suicidal person near you, don't be timid. Some of those contemplating suicide don't leave notes, but most leave clues. The strongest warning signs are verbal. Take comments such as "I can't go on," "Nothing matters anymore" or even "I'm thinking of ending it all" seriously.

Other common warning signs include:

- Depression or withdrawal
- Behaving recklessly
- Getting affairs in order or giving away valued or sentimental possessions

- Showing marked changes in behavior, attitude or appearance
- Abusing drugs or alcohol
- Being confronted by a major loss or life-changing event

With a person who is intent on suicide, try to establish some rapport. "I can see you are in a lot of pain." "I want to understand how you feel." "I am concerned for you." "What happened recently that made you feel this way?" If he won't cooperate, try to get as much of the following information as possible for the police or the 911 operator. Ask questions about things that might be important to him. What will happen to your dog or some cherished possession or person. Ask him about the sadness he will cause his relatives or friends.

Try to keep the person in sight. If you can't, get as much of the following information as you can so you can direct a 911 operator:

"What is your plan?"

"How do you plan to do it?"

"What is your phone number?"

"Where are you now?" (Get cross streets)

"Where are you headed?" (Find out his route of travel)

"What kind of car are you driving?"

"What are you wearing?"

"Who will be most hurt if you leave?"

For phone help, call:

      1-800-784-2433 or 1-800-SUICIDE

      1-800-273-8255 or 1-800-273-TALK

      Military
      1-800-273-8255 or 1-800-273-TALK (press 1)

      Spanish
      1-800-273-8255 or 1-800-273-TALK (press 2)

SERIES C: Topic 11

Fixing on the Fly

A little fix early on is usually more effective than a big fix later. By the time you realize you have goofed, you tend to want to hide from it and then get distracted by other pressures. It's no wonder you may end up making the same mistakes over and over!

In life, as in golf, you don't get to play any of your holes over again, but you can use the moment to improve your game. When the best golfers make bad shots, they "fix them on the fly." You can, too.

Procedure

1. Pause and block out all your distractions.

2. Observe what you did wrong as if from outside yourself.

3. Decide what you should have done.

4. Visualize yourself doing that, and the result you expect from that action.

The stakes you play for in life are more important than how well you play golf. You are playing for your life. The more you improve your ability to observe and explain what is happening and what you could have done better, the easier life will be for you and your loved ones. When you can fix your social blunders on the spot, it demonstrates to your friends and family your quality as a person and how you value them.

Today you couldn't buy word processing software without the spell-check feature, which literally fixes on the fly. Unless your goofs are way off the mark, you can watch your computer clean up your spelling, punctuation and grammar mistakes while you continue to type. Spell check never judges you or complains about your attitude, and it never brings up your previous failures, so it is never a threat to you. If you don't agree with it, it lets you proceed in your own way (and at your own peril).

> **The moment you goof, pause long enough to think of what you should have done. Then lock that solution into your memory by visualizing it producing the result you desire.**

When you are asked a question or get into a situation where you need time to come up with a response that will recognize the thinking of all parties, you might say "I need time to think." or, "My initial response is _____, but I need more information or insight before I decide where I'll stand on the issue."

The number of times you have to correct a child before he complies, tunes you out or rebels depends on all the corrections that have gone before. If you have allowed behaviors to grow into habits, you will be required to use more authority to enforce your will. The earlier and friendlier you can make your corrections, the fewer and milder they will have to be.

Spouting off, unloading and shooting from the hip are all reactions that can make you feel good at the moment but damage your relationships. When you and everyone else knows your responses will take into account the interests of all concerned, your friends and children will be more willing to open up to you and go with your judgment.

Fixing on the fly with others doesn't mean you respond quickly. Try not to feel like you need to render a decision or reaction immediately, or that taking more time to decide will make you seem less sure of yourself. Take the time you need to make your best judgment. The more often you are right, the easier it is for others to rely on your decisions.

SERIES C: Topic 12

Winning

A stand-up comedian wins when he gets applause. The applause you need most could be love, approval or praise. Are you going at life in a way you are likely to get the kind of applause that would mean the most to you?

People don't root for the guy who is disappointed with himself. They root for the underdog who is genuine, reliable, caring and so focused on finding a way to win that he's unaware of himself or his limitations. That's because he is a winner.

Even if you never place or finish in an event, you can be a winner in life. Winning has nothing to do with what you accomplish— it's about your character, what you value, how trustworthy you are and the extent to which you take other people's needs into consideration as you work toward your goals.

Being a winner is using the capabilities you have effectively, and loving what they produce.

Why does the other guy always seem to get the job, the girl, the good tickets and the fancy car—while you don't?

- He arrived first and came "ready to play."
- He wanted it more and tried harder.
- He worked "smarter."
- He learned what he needed to know.

- He was more persistent.
- He had tried and failed numerous times and learned from his mistakes.
- He got advice from someone who had already succeeded.
- He gave up all the things he could have been doing, while he prepared.

Winning requires persistence, a running start, keeping your eye on the ball and expecting success. It is being aware of and prepared to react to all the things that could go wrong, as well as all the things that can't go wrong but somehow do.

Imagine you are in a dirt bike race, and the fastest way to the finish requires you to make it up a steep hill. You are on the gas, and because you are looking uphill for the right route, you fail to notice a rock on the edge of the path. You hit it and land hard in the bushes. You now have bent handlebars, no front brake, a hurt shoulder and shaken confidence. You will now have to take an easier route and finish in the back of the pack. Some of the "rocks" that cause your life to stall or go backward, or that put you out of the race include:

- Early marriages or marrying the wrong person.
- Having children too early in life.
- Overspending.
- Substance abuse.
- Proceeding with inadequate thought or preparation.
- Choosing fun now over long-term benefits.
- Not taking education seriously.
- Job hopping.
- Not respecting rules or authority.

- Being reckless with your health or body.
- Not doing things when they should be done.
- Not trying hard enough.
- Lack of self-control.
- Attitude, self-pity, pride, or arrogance.
- Indifference to what is right or wrong.
- Neediness, impatience, envy, or laziness.
- Hopelessness or selfishness.

To earn millions, professional baseball pitchers will spend years replacing good habits with better ones. That's how some of them can throw a ball 100 miles an hour. They put everything they've got into every pitch.

Seeing your efforts succeed is the best motivator. "Nothing breeds success like success."

The events of the past can't keep you from being a winner in the future; being a winner depends entirely on what you do NEXT.

ASK YOURSELF

Which "win" have I wanted but never gone after?

What have I attempted that deserves another try?

What subject do I want to know everything about?

SERIES C: Topic 13

Willpower Tools

When you want to change yourself in important ways, or accomplish goals that will take a lot of hard work over a long period, make sure you have as many of the willpower tools helping you as you can.

When you have a sense of humor and an open mind, it takes a lot less willpower to change. Change is the process by which you find your power and your path to a more exciting future. It moves the task of changing from work to pleasure.

See how the tools below show up in the examples that follow.

Tools

1. Your most powerful tool is you. Keep yourself fully charged with love, appreciation, curiosity and self-confidence.

2. Get and keep your life right and you will do whatever it takes to protect it.

3. Work toward a solution rather than away from the problem.

4. Devote 95% or more of your thoughts to finding and visualizing solutions, and 5% or less to the problem.

5. If you act "as if" you can do something and proceed, you will grow into the role.

6. Pick goals that excite you. Goals that are boring, unrealistic or too hard (in your mind) will give you very little willpower to achieve them.

7. Criticizing yourself or wishing you were different puts pressure on you, makes achieving your objective harder and reduces the joy of succeeding.

8. To keep from being overwhelmed by large tasks, divide them into smaller steps with frequent rewards and diversions.

9. Enjoy where you are in the process while visualizing how your life is going to be when you achieve complete success.

10. Finding the help or coaching you need early in the process is efficient; waiting to get help until you have developed bad habits or are about to give up is not.

11. Increase your creativity by keeping a grateful, inquisitive outlook. (see Topic A-7 at GetLifeRight.com.)

12. Have a cause or a purpose for your life that is more important than you are.

13. Be curious, mentally flexible and ready to try things other people's way.

14. Assume your opinion of what you can't do is only a prejudice that you can overcome under the right conditions; then create those conditions.

15. Do what you can do where it is the most satisfying and/or has the most potential for advancement.

Examples

A woman "acted as if" she could be comfortable in a crowd, and she grew into that role. Her companion thought he couldn't function in a crowd and he grew into that role. (Tool #5)

A woman who wouldn't work a little harder to make 3% more money had no trouble working twice as hard to start her own business and make twice as much. (Tool #6)

The lone survivor in a German concentration camp was a man who believed he needed to stay alive so there would be someone to tell the story of what happened. Having that purpose saved his life. (Tool #12)

A woman who had tried unsuccessfully to get off drugs was able to quit "cold turkey" when she found out she was pregnant and knew her drug habit threatened the health of her baby. She finally had a cause that was more important than herself. (Tool #12)

The sole survivor of a plane crash ate bugs, grass and roots while he waded through snake-infested water. He was very imaginative in finding his way out of the Everglades. With nobody there to lean on, complain to, con or impress, he found he could do just about anything. (Tool #14)

A college student studied accounting so he could eventually take over his dad's practice. Work was drudgery until a client asked him for help with his restaurant that was failing. During college he had worked at a very successful dinner house. His ideas caused his client's restaurant to prosper. Today he creates new restaurants in good times and saves failing restaurants in hard times. (Tool #15)

ASK YOURSELF

Which tools have I been overlooking?

Which challenge am I ready for now?

How does the way I normally see myself hold me back?

SERIES C: Topic 14

Longevity and Health

How much life do we get? The average life expectancy in the United States is 78.8 years. (It's higher for females). By age 20 we will have had a billion heartbeats. Our DNA gets copied into every new cell. Like a picture degrades when it is reproduced over and over, our DNA cells do, too, according to what some researchers believe. The changes are too small to measure, but each one may affect some body function or feature.

Whatever the process is, it sets the outside limit of how long we can live. In spite of this, our DNA supports much more life than that. The amount of life that is estimated to be lost due to poor lifestyle choices can be as much as 30%.

Your cells are dying and have to be removed as new cells are replacing them. All your muscle cells must be replaced three times a year, your blood cells quarterly and half your bone cells annually. Vigorous exercising cleanses your body of weak, inactive and dead cells so that your new cells can attach to healthier surfaces.

It's important to "work out" your mind just as you would your body to keep it in top shape. Brains, like veins, become inflexible and lose their capabilities if they are not used vigorously. The following approaches are recommended for you in order to maintain both mental and physical vitality:

Shed stress—letting go of worry, depression, anger, resentment and fear is vital to your overall well being. People subjected to long-term stress are at greater risk of high blood pressure and stroke.

Develop close relationships—recent studies have placed socialization above exercise as the most important ingredient in living longer.

Exercise regularly—it offers an immediate boost to your spirits and energy! Experts now believe your activity should make you breathe hard and perspire for 45 minutes or more and include periods where you use all your strength. Stronger muscles metabolize food better. Strength-training exercises build muscles but don't have to be performed as often as conditioning exercises. Get an OK from your doctor before you begin any new exercise regimen.

All TV shows have commercials every quarter and half-hour. They are long enough for you to do a set of push-ups, sit-ups, squats, lunges, or your favorite exercise. One set would not normally cause you to perspire enough to require a shower.

Work your heart—ideally, when you exercise, your heart should beat at 60 percent of its capacity for most of an hour, three or more days a week. Using a heart-rate monitor helps you stay interested. Frequent bursts to 80% or more of your capacity are recommended. Every two weeks or so, schedule a workout that is substantially longer and harder than usual. Exercise cleanses your blood, veins and body, allowing new cells to operate in ideal conditions. When your blood is flowing freer, your heart works easier all the time—even when you aren't exercising.

The rule of thumb for determining your maximum heart rate is 220 minus your age. The formula suggests we lose one beat per year from our maximum rate. Those who work their hearts vigorously and consistently usually have standing heart rates below those of most people their age.

After age 40 we begin to lose muscle mass. Muscles process food more efficiently than fat, so if we eat the same amount of food, over time we will gain fat. Some of it will grow within the walls of our arteries, which usually increases our blood pressure. If we get more sedentary, we will tire more easily and our hearts will have to work harder.

Get your friends or family involved. Vary your program and cross-train. Take vacations that include hiking, skiing, biking or kayaking. Exercise rewards you with endorphins that make you feel good. It's your body's way of thanking you and encouraging you to stay fit.

Nutrition—it is easy to mistake anxiety for hunger. Those who manage these sensations by eating tend to grow; those who manage them by exercising tend to be stronger and live longer.

Hydration—typically a man needs about 13 cups of fluid of all kinds every day (9 cups for a woman), plus

16 ounces for each hour of continuous exercise. Water is best.

Alcohol causes you to lose water. Limit your alcohol intake to two servings in a day, and don't drink every day. Limit your drinks to 1.5 ounces of liquor, 10 ounces of wine or two regular-size beers. Women who weigh less than 160 pounds are advised to drink less.

When you have a bad diet and a lack of exercise, the cholesterol in your blood can cause plaque to build up in your arteries. It is detectable in people as young as age 20 and is a leading cause of heart attacks.

Life Expectancy Formula

The current formula at Northwest Mutual/Minnesota State Retirement System is now digital at **http://media.nmfn.com/tnetwork/lifespan**. The manual formula below is older but still convenient, and the outcomes are not much different:

1.   Start with the number 72.

2.   If you are male, subtract 3.

3.   If you are female, add 4.

4.   If you live in an urban area with the population over 2 million, subtract 2.

5.   If a grandparent lived to age 85 or over, add 6.

6.   If all four grandparents lived to age 80 or over, add 6.

7. If either parent died of a stroke or heart attack before 50, subtract 4.

8. If any parent, brother or sister under age 50 has (or had) cancer or a heart condition or has diabetes, subtract 2.

9. As an individual, do you earn over $60,000 a year? If so, subtract 2.

10. If you finished college, add 1.

11. If you have a graduate or professional degree, add 2 more.

12. If you are 65 or over and still working, add 3.

13. If you live with a spouse or friend, add 5. If not, subtract 1 for every 10 years alone since age 25.

14. If you work behind a desk, subtract 3.

15. If your work requires heavy physical labor, add 3.

16. If you exercise strenuously (tennis, running, etc.) five times a week for at least half an hour, add 4; if two or three times a week, add 2.

17. Do you sleep more than 10 hours each night? Subtract 4.

18. Are you intense? Aggressive? Easily angered? Subtract 3.

19. Are you easy-going and relaxed? Add 3.

20. Are you happy? Add 1. Unhappy? Subtract 2.

21. Have you had a speeding ticket in the last year? Subtract 1.

22. Do you smoke more than two packs a day? Subtract 8. One

or two packs? Subtract 6. One-half to one pack? Subtract 3.

23. Do you drink the equivalent of two drinks of hard liquor a day? Subtract 1.

24. Are you overweight by 50 pounds or more? Subtract 8. By 30 to 50 pounds? Subtract 4.

25. By 10 to 30 pounds? Subtract 2.

26. If you are a man over 40 who gets annual checkups, add 2.

27. If you are a woman and see a gynecologist once a year, add 2.

28. If you are between 30 and 39, add 2.

29. If you are between 41 and 49, add 3.

30. If you are between 51 and 69, add 4.

31. If you are over 71, add 5.

Now compare your score to the national averages for people who are reasonably healthy, between the ages of 25 and 65 shown below.

Age Now	Male	Female
20–29	71.2	77.8
30–39	71.3	77.9
40–49	73.5	79.4
50–59	76.1	79.0
60–69	80.2	83.6
70–79	85.9	87.7
80–90	90.0	91.1

ASK YOURSELF

What exercise regimen will work best for me?

How can I learn more about eating better?

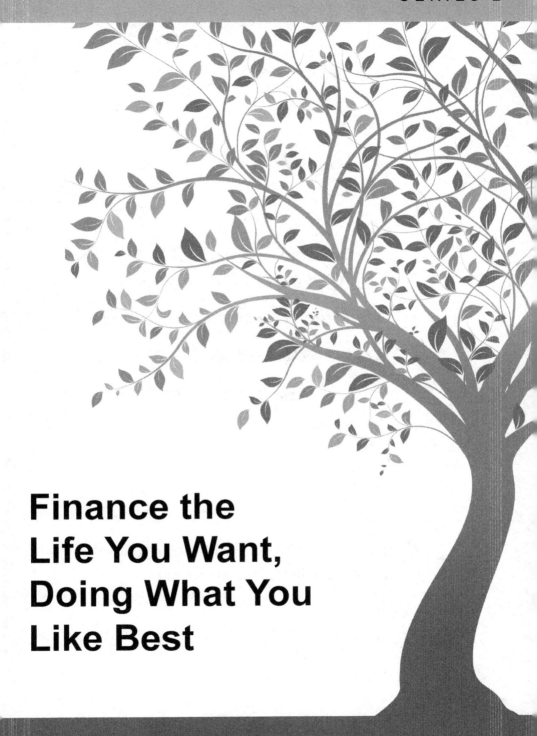

Finance the Life You Want, Doing What You Like Best

Keep your plan fresh for accumulating the amount you'll need for living, retirement and emergencies. Start saving now.

Read or download wealth-building Topics at GetLifeRight.com/Resources

SERIES D: Topic 1

Choosing a Career Path

Match your ambition to the work that will be most fulfilling. Be aware of how the job you are about to take (and all those that follow) will fit into your Plan for your life and retirement. Put your trust in your own ability. Your employer could go broke, sell out, shut down your department or close the month after you are hired.

Your security isn't found in the company you work for, but in what you know and can do.

Make sure the jobs you pick work toward your long-term needs. That will usually require a sequence of jobs. If the job you have doesn't contribute to your game plan for life, look for a job that does, but learn as much as you can at every job you hold.

Any job can be the right job if you can learn enough of the right things while you are there. One man was embarrassed because he dug ditches for $10 an hour. His co-worker turned down a different job making more money so he could dig ditches. It was important for the second man because he wanted to become a landscape designer and needed to know how to build walls and foundations. He showed up early, stayed late, and asked a lot of questions. When the job was over, the contractor asked him to stay on and assume more responsibility.

There are plenty of opportunities for people who could never get hired for an executive-level job. A lot of people are unable to see any future in what they are doing, but Jim did. Everyone envied Jim because he was doing extremely well with his vending machine business. What they didn't know was that because Jim was poor and uneducated, he worked for less than the minimum wage for years.

When the owner of the business died, nobody would buy his business because his machines were old and located in places where few drinks were sold. Since Jim was the only person who knew the business and he had been reliable, the owner's children sold Jim the business with no money down.

Over the next 15 years Jim and his family went without. They put every penny they could save into the business. He bought all new machines and got them all into profitable locations. Jim never wanted to service those old machines, and especially not for so long, but it trained him well for the best job he ever had—being the owner of his own company. Had he not been patient, he could still be moving from job to job.

Business Insights to Consider

Jobs at big companies are usually more rigid and clearly defined. This makes it easier for the company to compare your performance to that of many others.

Small companies tend to be less stable and less structured, and they tend to build jobs around the people they have. That allows creative people to assume responsibility sooner.

Get computer skills. Without them you will be considered illiterate for most jobs.

If you don't know the kind of work you want to do, begin anywhere and let that job guide you. It is easier to get a job when you already have a job.

Know how much you can make. Employers tend to exaggerate the amount of money you can earn, especially in commissions.

Look for careers on the Internet, in the library or bookstore, at job fairs, or on magazine racks. Drive through industrial areas and apply at businesses that seem prosperous.

New jobs are created around new concepts. Watch for new trends that interest you and for ways to "get in on them" while they are still hot.

Network—let everyone know you are looking for a job, especially those who work in industries that interest you.

Write your contact information and a few words about your capabilities or interests on small papers like business cards. Give them to your friends to hand out if they hear of any job opportunities. Carry these with you at all times.

When you reach the point at your current job where you're learning fewer and less-important things, start looking for a better job. Try not to leave before you have another better job lined up. And try to leave on good terms with everyone. Never burn bridges or unload. Give your employer enough notice to find a replacement—two weeks is customary. Also, ask your boss for a letter of recommendation at this time.

ASK YOURSELF

What can I learn at this job that will make my future better, easier or safer?

Does the experience or knowledge I am learning here improve my résumé for the type of job I want next?

Does it make my progress look slow or fast?

How can I use the things I can learn here to help me create my own business

SERIES D: Topic 2

Find the Most Satisfying Work

Making enough money to pay for the life you want often requires you to have a series of three to five jobs where you learn and earn more with each new job. Before you take any new job, make sure it will help you transition to a better job in a year or two, and that the better job will help you land an even better job a couple of years later.

To reduce the pressure on you and to get the most out of every interview, treat each one as a rehearsal for the one that follows.

Question Your Way to the Work That Fits You Best

Here are some good questions to ask yourself; jot down your responses:

- Where can I work that I can buy or earn an interest in the company?
- What am I best at right now?
- What could I learn to do better?
- What would be the most satisfying?
- Which type of work would make me the happiest?
- Which job would allow me to use my capabilities best?

- What kind of job will allow me to work around or help me with my weaknesses?
- What would be better for me now: schooling, training or work experience?
- What type of job can I do part time or from home while my kids are young?
- What have I done that I've received praise for?
- Which products/services interest me?
- What is the easiest for me to learn?
- How can I make the fastest progress?
- Where will I be needed most?
- Where can I make the most important contribution?

Make Your Application Fit the Job and Company You Are Applying To

Read every word of their website and talk to some of their customers, suppliers and employees. Show that you know what the company does, and that you have some knowledge of the job that is available and the work you'd like to grow into there.

Show that the job is a good fit for your career goals and that it would motivate you to make an important contribution to the company.

Provide, and/or have rehearsed, explanations for the following:

- ☑ Job changes that don't show advancement or don't appear logical
- ☑ Time that can't be accounted for
- ☑ A history of short-term jobs

☑ Jail time, drug problems

☑ Medical issues and special needs

If you are applying for an important job, make sure you are proud of your credit history and everything on your Facebook account—because a prospective employer will check.

Help the employer verify your information by providing accurate names, addresses and phone numbers of all your former employers and references.

Practice

- Get several blank application forms—or make copies of the original—so you can practice on them. Complete the final application as professionally as possible. When the employer asks you to put your information on a form, do it; but also attach a copy of your qualifications written your way.

- If you can include an email address for yourself, it will suggest to the employer that you are computer literate.

- When you apply for work, be sure to bring along your résumé and all the details of your previous employment. While assembling this information, think of the questions you will be asked and rehearse your answers. Rewrite your résumé several times over several days. Have others read and correct each draft.

- Do a final review of the application, looking for and correcting:

  ☑ Incomplete information

  ☑ Smudges, wrinkles, errors and corrections

  ☑ Poor grammar, misspellings and sloppy handwriting

Show Determination

Follow up your interview with a thank-you phone call to the person who interviewed you. Ask about the status of your application. If you don't get the job, reapply again soon.

Which type of work will move you toward the type of job you will need to pay for the life you want to have?

How can you show how clever and energetic you can be at the work they have available?

Have you been going after just any job, or the job you want most?

If you are not hired, you can take positive action: Now that you know what the company needs, you can take two classes and reapply for a better job than the one you didn't get this time.

SERIES D: Topic 3

Marketing Yourself

Jobs with the most future go to those whose lives are trending in the right direction. Accomplishments that are close together act like springboards to further advancements with more potential. Flat spots in your career tend to limit you to opportunities with limited potential.

Prepare a cover letter with three short paragraphs. Try to have it show the trend of your life, your capabilities and your desirability as an employee. Base what you write on your present skills, but show the things you are doing to improve your qualifications. Show how the goals of the company are a good match for your career goals. Have others read your words and revise them until you love them. Attach this to any job application you fill out, even if they don't ask for it.

Develop a Marketing Campaign

- Contact five prospective employers every day.
- Go on at least one interview a week.
- Ask those around you to watch for the type of job you want.
- Give others your contact information, the type of work you want and your best qualifications on a paper the size of a business card they can give to others.

- Post your résumé on various Internet websites, including that of the Employment Development Department.

- After you have given notice, but before or shortly after you leave an employer, get a letter of recommendation. (The person in that company who knew your work may be gone next week.)

- Put copies of this letter of recommendation with every application you make. Include references on your quality as a person from teachers, neighbors or agencies you've volunteered with.

- Make your résumé and application forms as professional as possible.

- Consider your appearance; tattoos, piercings, hairstyle, clothing, language, attitude, tardiness and poor posture can hurt your chances.

Homework

- Learn to use the computer.
- Search the Internet for companies that interest you.
- Read industry publications to learn about the competitors, trends and outlook for the industry that interests you.
- Discover which companies will train you best.
- Look for companies that are new, advertising, growing or in the news.
- Look into new industries where new jobs are being created.
- Learn about nearby businesses.
- Get a better job at your current workplace.
- Go to work for companies that buy from, supply or compete with the company you work for now.
- Search the Internet on sites like Google Job Search, Monster Jobs, Yahoo Hot Jobs and the Employment Development Department (EDD) job bank.

Non-Traditional Jobs

Internships—if there is something you think you would like to do, find a company that does it and work for them free for a while. You'll be able to figure out if this is the field for you. If the company is impressed, it may create a job for you. At the very least, you'll gain some experience.

Start-ups—work part time for a company that can't afford a full-time employee.

Benefits—consider working for benefits such as health insurance, free travel, access to events or some ownership of the business.

Flex-time—an employer may allow you two choices between working schedules. Many sales jobs can be done from home, as in outside sales. Working an evening or night shift allows you to take schooling, prepare for a better job, start a business or be there when the kids get home from school.

Self-employment—your options include buying your own business or franchise, selling products on commission or starting your own business.

Travel—if you are not tied down with family needs, you can work abroad or on a cruise ship or in a place where you can get extra pay because the conditions are remote or demanding.

Commissions—find a product you appreciate and that you can sell easily.

Swap meets—create a business selling something you have access to or really like.

Move—be willing to relocate to another city or state.

Ownership—if you can sustain yourself, work for ownership in the business of your employer or become a partner.

Night shifts—get a night job that can pay the bills while you train or search for the work you want during the day.

ASK YOURSELF

How can I customize my résumé and cover letter to fit the company and job I am applying for?

What does it tell me about me?

What does it reveal that I need a ready answer for?

SERIES D: Topic 4

Applying for Work

It is only logical that a potential employer will see the quality of effort and planning you have put into your life from your résumé or application and assume you will bring the same qualities to your job.

Your employment application can reveal more about you than you realize. It can tell others:

- You haven't done much or you progress slowly.
- You are not observant or haven't tried hard enough.
- You are not persuasive.
- You don't organize your life well.
- You have poor English, can't write, or lack computer skills.
- You can't make up your mind.
- You have no long-range-planning skills.

Those who have made smart moves quickly are more likely to get the jobs where they can advance quickly. People who don't seem to be concerned about their future get the jobs with the least potential for advancement.

It is likely you will have to compete with people who have already done the type of work you are seeking and have prepared well for that job. But don't let that discourage you. Your employer may need a person who has more social skills or who can work for less money or who could be a coordinator rather than a technician. By reading up on the company before the interview, maybe you could be hired for a job better than the one advertised. Look on the company's website and talk to its customers, competitors and suppliers. Maybe you can teach the owner something about his company that he has not been aware of.

Be honest and straightforward about your skills. If you can convince the employer you are eager to learn and work hard, you may be able to secure a job that you aren't quite qualified for.

If you are applying for a more important job, and your interviewer starts to ask questions dealing with matters other than your job skills, it could be a good sign. He is trying to find out if you would be suited for interaction with customers, sales or management. He'll want to know:

- Your knowledge of his customers and how to work with them.
- Ways you helped your past employers.
- How likeable you are and how you would fit in.
- Your ability to handle the unexpected.

Your attitude, dependability, adaptability and people skills are valuable. In many work environments, finding the person who is right for the job can be more important than hiring the person who is most technically qualified.

If an interviewer has told you that you don't meet his criteria, then before you get to the door, ask as many questions as you can about the company or its needs. It will make you smarter if you reapply, or maybe there's a different job in the company that would be a better match for you.

Try to get a job that will allow you to work in your most productive way. Some people do best in groups, some alone, some with an audience, some with interruptions, some with noise or in confusion, some at another's pace, some in the morning or in the evening and some where they aren't being compared directly to other employees. Figure out how you work best, and find a job where those conditions exist.

Before you start a new job, try to determine how far you can advance with it and how much you can improve your skills and assume responsibilities. If you haven't already done so, compute the most money you can make in Year 1, Year 3, and Year 20 at this job. If that isn't enough to fund the way you want to live, think of that job as a stepping-stone job. Then start preparing for and looking for one that will adequately fund your lifestyle goal.

ASK YOURSELF

Who can I get to show me how to search the Internet for jobs?

Who can tell me how to learn about a prospective employer on the Internet?

What classes could I sign up for that will make me more qualified for the job or line of work I want?

SERIES D: Topic 5

Positioning Yourself in the World

Often the ability to do something well is not as important as where you do what you can do.

Many jobs that have no future can require as much effort as those that offer great opportunity. If you take work on an assembly line, you could be setting yourself up for a low-paying job that is repetitive, where you can be replaced easily, and where you may have no way to progress.

A janitor who works in a train station is less likely to get a shot at a job with potential than if he works for a growth company like Apple, Google, or Microsoft.

> **The best jobs are usually either hard to find or so obvious that they are taken by insiders. Find work close to the type of work you want do. That way, you can see the opportunities as they and have a better idea of how to take advantage of them.**

The better you know where you want your life and your career to go, the more likely you will be to know when and where to find the job opportunities that will fill your need, or that become available.

Pay attention to how the job you are about to take is going to help you get the job that follows it and moves you toward your long-term goals.

If you were auctioning off your services, you would not get top dollar for them unless you auction them where the audience is large and affluent and seeks what you have to offer.

If you sell your own paintings, as soon as you stop painting you are out of business. If you had the rights to reproduce a picture, you could sell many copies of it, or give others the right to sell it for you. Manufacturers, inventors, authors, singers, and artists all sell multiple copies of what they do. Every copy that sells multiplies the return on the time or money spent producing or selling it.

How much money do you think you would have made if you were the person who invented sticky notes?

The time to start positioning yourself for retirement is when you graduate from high school.

Stunning Examples of Positioning

The following occurred in one of the biggest subway terminals during a busy time of day. For 45 minutes, Joshua Bell—considered by many to be one of the best violinists in the world—played some of his most intricate pieces on a violin worth $3.5 million. With the exception of a few people who paused to listen for a while, his efforts were largely unappreciated. That same week, he packed a concert hall where the tickets cost $100 each.

In the Scottish hamlet where Susan Boyle grew up, she was taunted by the other kids a lot. That kept her close to home. When she reached adulthood she became the caregiver to her ailing mother. Her only outlet was to sing at church and social events near her home. When her mother died, Susan was approaching 50—hardly the time to launch a singing career. But she'd promised her mother that she'd sing, so she auditioned for Britain's Got Talent 2009. Within one week, her surprising audition got 1.3 million hits on YouTube! Her first CD was a best-seller. While her voice would have been appreciated anywhere, few would have ever heard it if she had not gotten it into a position where it could achieve its true potential.

At a Thanksgiving dinner on a military base where high school freshman Shauna Fleming was serving GIs, she realized soldiers need to be appreciated more. She decided to generate some thank-you notes. She and some friends came up with the name "A Million Thanks" for her campaign. Because she was so young, and the media liked the idea so much, she became an instant celebrity. She was on many national television programs and hundreds of radio programs. Within about four months, she was at the White House where she gave then-President George W. Bush the one-millionth thank-you note. With her idea and a lot of help from the high school she attended and many other volunteers, she delivered more than four million thank-yous. She had positioned herself where she could have the maximum impact with her idea and capabilities.

Do what you like best or can do best, and reposition yourself constantly until you love what you are doing and you are using your capabilities where they can do the most good for the greatest number of people.

ASK YOURSELF

Have I taken charge of my retirement yet?

Is the potential I am headed for enough, or am I settling?

How can I position myself for the best use of my skill set?

SERIES D: Topic 6

Crafting Abundance

The more resources you have at your disposal, the more you can accomplish with your capabilities. The more capable you are, the easier it is for you to accumulate wealth in all forms.

> **Your wealth is far more than your monetary assets such as money and possessions. It also includes your knowledge, capabilities, explanations, relationships, ethics, advantages and experiences.**

Thoughts, just like money, are assets. The right thoughts attract good people and creativity into your life and increase your advantages, capabilities and options.

Those who make the most of their existence use their wealth to earn, learn, bond, and help others. They make everything they do produce lasting value, and they reinvest what they receive in new things of lasting value. Ideally they invest some of their assets in things that will increase in value, where little of their personal effort is required, such as stocks, bonds, property, ideas and the futures of others. Do you remember Alexandra's lemonade stand? (See Topic C-3 at GetLifeRight.com). Her idea continues to raise money for kids with cancer, even though she has been gone for years.

When you have your life crafted properly, the more of your

abundance you use, the more it produces. You gain wealth by putting yourself in situations where you can learn and benefit from using your assets and capabilities to help others. You lose it when you are down on yourself, negative or unappreciative, or you stop crafting. Abundance enables you to experience the exhilaration of fulfillment and of performing near the limit of your capabilities.

Like everyone else, you have needs you must work toward fulfilling to be happy: to be free, to have knowledge, to be in control, to understand how things work, to own things, to do things, to be religious or spiritual, to be involved socially, to have close relationships, to be quiet or to be ambitious. But take care: Whenever you allow any one of your needs to become too strong, it diminishes the others; and the overall abundance of your life shrinks because it gets out of balance.

Wealth creation, in all its forms, requires long-term planning. It produces the pleasure of accomplishment, which stays with you always. It is far more satisfying than the temporary pleasure of immediate gratification, which has to be recreated over and over.

Good judgment in investing and personal finances requires a lot of thought over time. Read everything you can get your hands on, and from as many sources as possible. Start now. Here are two excellent resources:

> You can set out to get a job or to get wealthy. Learn the difference in the book *Rich Dad Poor Dad* (Robert Kiyosaki, www.richdad.com).

> For investing and personal finances, go to www.daveramsey.com.

ASK YOURSELF

Have I ever considered accumulating wealth in any form?

What's the most important thing I can start accumulating right away?

Of all the things I can do, which has the most growth potential?

SERIES D: Topic 7

Risk and Persistence

If you're like most people, you want to avoid risk, loss and harm; and that protects you, more often than not. But financially you'll reap the greatest rewards when you evaluate and take risks. Most success comes from working through the unknowns; living in vagueness, being at risk and managing your emotions. The easiest part of succeeding is doing the work. The hardest part is knowing the right field, sustaining yourself financially and emotionally long enough to become an expert and find the right opportunity.

What you fear doing or learning most is often a good indicator of what would be the most beneficial for you. When a teen boy is in the presence of a girl he feels is beyond his reach, he often gets tongue tied.

Your fear of the unknown is holding you back. When you shy away from the things you fear, your growth stops in that direction. When you go toward the unknown, as if it is a source of knowledge, growth, adventure and joy, you become more capable and self-assured.

There are risks involved in everything you do, and in everything you fail to do. You are always risking everything you have, but you probably don't realize it. Risks you don't take at the right time often force you to take greater risks in the future.

Your gift and your happiness could come from doing work that doesn't pay well. Not everyone is born with the skills necessary to become secure financially. But those who don't take charge of their finances live at risk and struggle constantly. If you take the following concepts to heart, you will do better.

Knowledge and judgment—a heart surgeon has gone to school for 20 years, reads extensively and limits his practice to just a few procedures so he can know everything about them. For a new procedure, he observes other doctors; he does lab work, assists many times, and confers with the doctors who performed the operation. Until he can perform it flawlessly, he is observed by experienced doctors. This careful process gives the new surgeon the confidence he needs to deal with life-and-death situations.

If you could get the same quality of coaching as the surgeon on any subject, there are thousands of things you could do that don't seem possible to you now. Learn everything you can in the direction you want your life to go, and study from the best teachers you can find.

Where the right coach is not available, you have to become your own coach and learn the consequences of all the moves you will need to make to succeed with your finances and your passion. If you don't set your goals high and trust you will grow into them, you will continue to settle for less than you can have or do.

For you to have the best options at every decision point of your life, and to reduce the risk in your decisions, you need to have as many assets stored up as possible. What you have accumulated in knowledge, relationships, possessions, emotional maturity and savings becomes your power. The more power you have, the less risk there is in your moves and the more opportunities you can take advantage of.

Insiders get most of the best jobs and investment opportunities. Do what you have to do to become an insider. If entry into that group is closed, do something else. Opportunities are more plentiful and accessible in smaller companies.

When a popular shopping center was built, it's obvious it should be there. But it wasn't obvious 30 years before, when it was lowland and the owner got it for a song. But he had to import dirt for years to make it level, and he spent 7 years coming up with the right tenants, 2 years getting permits and 2 years in construction. In many investments, you make your money when you buy, but you may keep investing and be patient to collect.

Having the long view is usually the fastest route to your most important goals. Mr. Longview doesn't know when his big opportunity will come along; he just knows "the harder he looks for it, the luckier he'll get." He also knows that the more he prepares, the more likely he'll be able to make the best use of the opportunities he gets. As early as high school he can begin to accumulate the skills and knowledge he will need to reach his farthest goals.

Mr. Longview works for 10 years in the industry where he plans to invest. He develops lots of friends in the business. He knows how they each make money. He finally sees a need and gets enough orders to convince a lender to lend him $100,000 for a machine that grinds metal into more usable scrap. He uses part of his savings for a down payment and the rest for working capital. He gets a line of credit from his bank.

In the following 20 years, Mr. Longview has bought six additional machines. They work around the clock; he doesn't. He has a manager who runs the business. He can hardly remember the sacrifices he made to get there; to him they were adventures. Mr. Longview was vulnerable early because he had to borrow heavily, but he was young enough at the time that he could have recovered if he failed.

Mr. Shortview felt the need to drive a late model car, and he lived larger than Mr. Longview for the first 15 years of his working life. The company he works for is not doing well, and there have been layoffs. His only significant asset is the equity in his house, and he won't be able to collect Social Security for years. He will be at financial risk for the rest of his life. The memory of his nice cars is not as satisfying as the vacations Mr. Longview now gets to take yearly.

**People who are afraid to change jobs could be
working for a company on the verge of failure.**

Persistence is how committed you are to finishing what you start. As Calvin Coolidge, the 30th President of the United States, said, "Nothing in the world can take the place of persistence. Talent will not; nothing is more common than unsuccessful men with talent. Genius will not; unrewarded genius is almost a proverb. Education will not; the world is full of educated derelicts. Persistence and determination alone are omnipotent."

ASK YOURSELF

What have I been fearful to pursue?

What do I need to learn next that will get me to the next level the fastest?

What would I love to do that will pay off for me financially in the long run?

Attract The People You'd Like to Be Like

Friendships: the reward you get
from giving yours away.

SERIES E: Topic 1

Making Friends

When you have friends you are close to, it makes you feel better about yourself. What good is success if you don't have friends to share your thoughts, struggles and accomplishments with? Without them, your life isn't providing you the nourishment you need to be happy and do your best. Loneliness can cause depression or alcoholism and can shorten your life.

The thoughts and mannerisms of your friends are contagious. If you are around them for a while, you'll catch what they've got. Your job is to be around people who will infect you with thoughts and ways that will make life better for you and your family.

> **Strangers are friends you haven't met. Friends are people who know all about you but like you anyway!**

If you don't have close friends, ask yourself:

- Do I come off as being unwelcoming, bored, or uninterested?
- Who have I been a good friend to?
- Whose friendship have I worked hard enough to earn?
- What am I saying or doing that is turning others off (attitude, hang-ups, sarcasm, manners, appearance, values and/or self-centeredness)?
- What could I be doing to attract them?

- How can I get to talk to more of them?
- Are my views too strong, dark, selfish, suggestive, liberal or conservative?

About Your Friends

- Who can you discuss anything with, get good advice from, and know your confidentiality will be respected?
- How many friends do you have who you can drop in on without notice anytime?
- How many people know and care about the hardships you have gone through in your job or personal life?
- How many people have you asked for their opinion on any important personal matter in the last month?
- How many people have asked you for your opinion on any important personal matter in the last month?
- Who is likely to give you the best advice on your career or on your personal life?
- Do you value the friendship of your family members more than your friendships with others?
- Who has given you the best advice in your life, so far?
- Do you share information about yourself, or hoard it?
- Do you use alcohol or drugs to fill in for the friends you don't have?
- How can I overcome my shyness and pick up the phone?
- How do you get close enough to talk?

Your Icebreakers

These conversation starters are likely to encourage others to talk with you. The list begins with the best:

- One or more small children
- A pet
- An unusual (not weird) activity
- A hobby that excites you
- A piece of sports equipment or clothing
- A carrying case for an instrument
- A logo on your shirt or jacket
- A cool camera
- A special vehicle
- A brochure or keychain device

Now that you get the idea, look for "icebreakers" in and around the people you want to meet.

Relationships need time to grow. Spend time with people you are likely to like, in ways that will allow you to see them over and over.

Spend Time with People You'd Like to Know

Parents who cheer for their kids at Little League all season become well acquainted with other families there.

Neighbors in new subdivisions bond easily as they landscape their yards.

Attending classes brings students together. Sign up for a course that appeals to you (golf, photography, etc.).

Ask someone for help or offer it (which suggests you are comfortable around that person).

Volunteer your skills for any good cause.

Use the Internet to find groups you can join that have activities you like. Meetup.com offers a wide variety of groups from Jeep clubs to movie buffs, and it has chapters all over the U.S.

> **When a person trusts you, you probably want to trust him or her back. When you trust others, most of them want to trust you back.**

Getting Your Act Together

Be happy.

Like yourself.

Shed your baggage.

Be first to break the ice and introduce yourself.

Try not to seem self-conscious.

Be engrossed (caught up) in an activity you find interesting.

Get involved in an activity others are already doing, or something you like to do or are good at.

Don't frighten people off by trying too hard or moving too fast to make a friend out of an acquaintance.

Minimize your solo activities like watching TV and surfing the Web.

Do activities where you interact with others; don't just be in the same place all the time.

Appear approachable. Smile and make eye contact.

When introduced to others, ask about their work or favorite activity to help you remember them.

If the other person can't remember your name, he might avoid you. Occasionally mention your name again (as if you wouldn't expect the other person to remember it).

Ask a few questions that are light, fun and impersonal to show you are friendly and feel comfortable around the person.

Act as if you are going to be liked.

Be patient and enjoy the other person's comments.

Encourage the other person to open up, and they will be unaware of whether you are nervous.

Act naturally. Expect a few goofs along the way as you improve this skill.

Never complain, exaggerate, brag or speak poorly of another person.

Practice on everyone you meet.

People will all get to know you eventually, so be yourself from the beginning. There is always a risk in making an attempt to get to know someone. You have to be willing to take chances if you want your world to grow through people you get to know.

There is a greater risk in allowing a person you don't know to have your contact information. An answering machine, a seldom-used email address, and meeting only in public places can help you keep newcomers at a distance until you are comfortable with them.

ASK YOURSELF

How can I act more comfortable with myself so others will be more comfortable around me?

What can I do to improve my appeal to others?

SERIES E: Topic 2

Keeping Friends

Having friends you feel close to makes you feel better about yourself. The absence of friends can lead you toward temptation and depression and dull your imagination, ambition and self-esteem.

A true friend is one who will do whatever it takes to make the other person feel good physically, mentally, emotionally and spiritually, and to show complete trust, forgiveness, acceptance and support for that person's well being and future.

Statistics show that people who have good friends live longer than those who don't.

Making someone else important to you is usually the best way to become important to them.

Ideas for Improving
Your Friendship Skills

Praise regularly—never pass up a chance to say something to other people that will make them feel better about their lives or what they are doing. Practice with everyone.

Take risks—nobody connects every time in trying to get to know someone better. We all get rejected sometimes.

Gain awareness—when something you say doesn't go over well, ask for clarity with a question like, "Something I said seems to have bothered you. Did I offend you?"

Be happy—people like being around people who are happy. Are your words and manner upbeat or depressing?

Listen—you can't influence other people unless you know how they think, and you can't learn if you aren't listening.

Give support—loyal friends help pull us through dark moods and self-pity. Who could use your help right now?

Be encouraging—criticism erodes a person's confidence; praise builds it. Encourage everyone.

Be tactful—let people adopt your ideas instead of trying to "sell" them. Help others draw their own conclusions instead of pushing them toward your viewpoint.

Use discretion—offer advice only when asked. Most people interpret unwanted advice as criticism and don't appreciate it. People are more likely to seek your counsel if they admire the way you are handling your own problems.

Smile—smile at others with your voice and body language, and they will smile back.

Be open—you encourage others to open up around you when you reveal your feelings. Also, make others feel they can offer advice without hurting your feelings.

Spend time—the amount of time you spend with a person is a good gauge of his importance to you.

Respect yourself—people can sense if you don't seem to like or respect yourself. Whether you realize it or not, your insecurity sends a message to others about how they should view you. Don't teach others to discount you.

Have a sense of humor—you can make others feel comfortable around you by dealing with disappointments and shortcomings with a good sense of humor.

Be trustworthy—always, and without being asked, keep the secrets and private thoughts of others to yourself.

Control your ego—pride issues are difficult to see in yourself and could limit your circle of friends.

Be presentable—if you don't maintain your appearance, you could be drawing negative attention to yourself.

Be generous—bring to your relationships at least as much as you are getting out of them.

Except when you receive sudden and devastating news, how you feel comes from how you think; not the other way around. Pleasant thoughts make you feel good; bad thoughts make you feel bad. The more you think it's okay to be unpleasant because of your misfortune or how hard you have had to work, the more you damage your relationships and make yourself feel bad.

> *Every time you have an angry thought, an unkind*
> *thought, a sad thought, or a cranky thought, your*
> *brain releases chemicals that make you feel bad.*
> —DANIEL G. AMEN, .D.

ASK YOURSELF

Does my Plan for life set aside enough time to find, develop and maintain friendships?

Do I have a true friend?

How do I let him/her know?

Which friendship would I most like to repair?

How good a friend am I to my family members?

SERIES E: Topic 3

Making Conversation

Talking is how we teach, and listening is how we learn.

To keep your conversations moving along, avoid asking closed-ended questions like "Do you like your job?" or "Do you live nearby?" which can be answered with a "yes" or "no." Ask open-ended questions such as:

What do you do for a living?

What's your opinion?

Can you tell me about...?

Why...?

How did you...?

How were you able to...?

What is your favorite...?

What do you do for fun?

Avoid giving one-word answers. Help the other person keep his side of the conversation going by giving him some things to ask you about.

Tips for Good Conversations

- Never say anything bad about yourself or another person.
- Practice being outgoing, warm and friendly with everyone until it is natural to you.

- Everyone knows something very interesting, and it will please you both if you can get them to talk about it.

- Practice finding the favorite interest of others using the fewest questions.

- Reveal personal information at the same rate your conversation partners reveal information about themselves.

- Proceed as if the other person is far more interested in hearing what they have to say than what you will have to say. Direct the conversation back to them as much as possible.

- When joining a group of people you don't know, start talking to the person who appears to be the most approachable or the one who seems most left out.

- Concentrate on getting to know two or three people better—learn what they do for fun and/or for work, or where they grew up.

- Remember your shyness makes the other person responsible for entertaining you. Put his comfort ahead of your own.

- You show appreciation when you let the speaker know you are paying attention. Occasionally ask a question like, "Can you tell me more about...?" or by redirecting the conversation back to his subject if he gets sidetracked.

- Before you change the subject to what you want to talk about, comment or ask the other person at least three questions about his current subject. (See Dave's "3 to 1 Rule" in the next section.)

- Make eye contact frequently.

- Be aware that most people get more information from your body language and tone than from your words.

- Compliment people for what they can do, have done, or are

trying to do.

- Words that exaggerate or are extreme, like "hate," "always," "never," "should," "can't," "only" and "have to," actually have less power than words that are accurate.
- If you can make someone feel better about herself she will feel better about you.
- Avoid trumping (having a bigger, better or more exciting tale to tell).
- Ask people about their feelings, their experiences, and their reactions.
- Don't finish other people's sentences, and don't start talking until they stop.
- Find out the other person's opinion on controversial subjects before you blurt out your own point of view—especially if you have strong feelings about the topic.
- When you find a good listener, be merciful. He is entitled to as much speaking time as you are.

ASK YOURSELF

What is my weakest communication skill?

Which of the changes above would help me most now?

Who will I practice my new skills with first?

SERIES E: Topic 4

Making Yourself Irresistible

You whisper a message to one person who whispers it to another. After fifteen people have participated, the original message is unrecognizable since no two people deliver a message exactly as they receive it. They each change it in some way.

Bad Listeners:

- Are preoccupied with what they are going to say instead of listening to the speaker.

- Quit listening if the speaker says something they disagree with.

- Hear only the statements that confirm their own opinions.

- Bend what is said to support what they already think.

- Use a comment the speaker has said to change the subject to their preferred topic.

- Start to tell their thoughts before the speaker has finished talking.

- Brag about their successes and victories.

- Talk too much (hence the saying, "There are some to whom there is nothing quite as lovely as the sound of their own voice").

- Deliberately distract the audience's attention away from the speaker (or say something that discredits him).

- Hijack control of the conversation so they can talk on topics of their choice.
- Speak with more emotion than is appropriate for the subject matter or situation.

Dave's 3 to 1 Rule

Ask **3** questions about what the other person is talking about, before switching **to** the **1** you want to talk about.

Good Listeners:

- Follow the 3 to 1 Rule.
- Temper their comments by finding out the other person's opinions before attempting to change the conversation to the subject they want to talk about.
- Make frequent eye contact without staring.
- Attempt to put the speaker at ease.
- Show genuine interest in the subject through their tone and body language.
- Wait for a conclusion instead of assuming what the speaker will say next.
- Show curiosity by using phrases such as, "What did you mean by... ?" "As I see it...," "So, what you're saying is..." and "How did you feel about that?"
- Try to get details without being personal or pushy.
- Repeat a comment or detail that the speaker has brought up in a previous conversation.

- Focus their undivided attention on the speaker.

People open up when their conversation is being enjoyed because:

- Good listeners make them feel more important.
- Their bodies produce more endorphins, the feel-good hormone.

ASK YOURSELF

As others are telling me something they have experienced, am I normally formulating questions about their topic or preparing to share an experience I have had on a related subject that would be more interesting to me?

What single question is most likely to get a person talking about what they like most?

What question could someone use to get me talking about my favorite subject?

SERIES E: Topic 5

Likability Skills

Find good in everyone you encounter and let them know what you've found.

Having good friends makes you feel that the world will like your ideas and efforts. What could be more encouraging? Attracting good friends tells you that you are being the type of person that people find appealing. Have people been seeking out your friendship?

Here are some ideas for improving your likability:

- All behavior has a purpose. Why are you doing what you are doing? Why are they doing what they are doing?
- Act as if others will be able to see your true intentions in what you say and do.
- You can reduce the number of arguments you get into by refusing to be upset with those who matter to you.
- Help others out of the kindness of your heart, without expecting repayment.
- People appreciate you more if you act less like a coach and more like a fan.
- Seek to understand before being understood.
- Show trust by sharing your feelings.
- Give everyone the benefit of the doubt until they prove themselves unworthy.

- If asked for your advice, use cans instead of shoulds.

- Most people would rather make their own mistakes than be constantly cautioned and prodded.

- Don't present your ideas or arguments too forcefully.

- When asked for constructive criticism, try to get the person to come up with his own answer by asking him questions. Stick to the issues he raises.

- When issues get heated, reduce the tension or leave the scene until you can handle the matter calmly.

- When a person overreacts, his response may have nothing to do with you or the issue at hand (unless you were responsible). Let the matter go.

- Present your recommendations as ideas for consideration, not for immediate acceptance.

- Before you react to explosive situations, pause, calm your emotions and seek clarification. Deliver your input when you are at peace with your position on the subject. (Warning—it may take days to get there.)

- When problem solving, keep your solutions focused on fixing the issue, not the person.

- With sensitive subjects, it's best to learn the other person's position before sharing any strong personal opinions.

- Don't let misunderstandings linger; mend your fences by fixing on the fly (see Topic C-11 at GetLifeRight.com).

- Pay close attention to your conversation partner's body language, especially when discussing issues you feel strongly about. If he is tuning you out or trying to avoid you, you have probably been too forceful or droning on.

- Even your best arguments and most clever thoughts won't be persuasive if your listener has "checked out."

- If you allow yourself to be driven by authority, duty or ambition, and you demand those things from those around you, they will leave at their first opportunity.

- "Resentment is like taking poison and hoping the other person dies. "You always pay a greater price for those emotions than the person you are angry with. Often that person has no idea why you are acting as you are. A negative attitude can cause you to make bad explanations about yourself, others, the world or your place in it.

- Get Life Right can inspire and show anyone the life to aim for, but those with profound systemic thought, emotional or behavioral problems such as insecurity, inferiority, ego, anger, judging, blaming, anxiety, control, fault finding, withdrawing, lying or cheating and other dependencies need additional help. These conditions require accurate diagnosis and diligent effort to overcome.

- If any of these behaviors are standing between you and the full enjoyment of your life, family or friends, make it your priority to read about your condition and find the right counselor.

ASK YOURSELF

Which new communication skill could I use on my boss, spouse or child?

What is my best social skill? Which of my skills needs the most improvement?

About the Relationship Series

The relationship ideas in this book work quickly and last for those who are stable and conscientious and have the best interests of their partners, friends and associates at heart. The relationship gains made by anyone can be short lived if one or both of the parties to a relationship have profound emotional, behavioral, thinking or dependency issues.

These conditions represent massive risks to all relationships, especially marriage. Neither party should enter a marriage until both understand the nature and depth of these problems and are willing to risk the consequences. Caution: The judgment of those willing to proceed in the face of these issues may be compromised by inferiority, insecurity or other issues of their own.

Diagnosing and healing from these conditions will happen faster and more completely for those who can find and open up to the right skillful counselor.

Some resources we like will be listed as Resources at GetLifeRight.com.

Improve Your Relationships and Marriage

Love is the joy you share when you
can both let your spouse's way
become your way.

SERIES F: Topic 1

Relationship Tools

Even when both people want to do everything they can to have a good relationship, feelings still get bruised.

Often the way you say something can be more harmful than what you say.

Some Basics

Keep your voice, tone, and emotional volume turned down as low as possible.

Always seek to understand before being understood.

Before you bring up a controversial subject, ask yourself, "How can I phrase this so no part of it can be taken the wrong way?"

Make sure you know what the other person intended before you retaliate. Ask something like "Can you rephrase that?" or "Did you mean to suggest that...?

How and when you open a subject usually has a big bearing on getting your point across; wait for the right timing to get started.

You can't expect others to reveal their innermost feelings unless you have made sure they are positive they will be treated with respect and their feelings kept private.

Always leave a safe way for you and the other person to revisit a sensitive subject in the future.

Don't try to fix an additional problem during a nice outing or celebration, or while making up from a previous difficulty.

As much as possible present ideas for consideration—not for immediate action.

When people react too forcefully to a situation, it usually suggests a much bigger issue is bothering them on the same or a different subject. If you can gently get them to reveal what that problem is, it's helpful; otherwise, let them tell you in their own time. You may not be able to find a permanent solution to the initial problem until you deal with the hidden problem.

When the topic you want to discuss is likely to be sensitive, tell the other person in advance that you want his input on the subject. It may be good to let him choose the time for the discussion.

When it is necessary to correct people, first reassure them (let them know this is not something that is going to damage your relationship), tell them what you have to say, and then reassure them again.

People feel betrayed when you get them to reveal personal information about themselves before they were ready to give it. Let them reveal their information in their own way and time.

When someone else is talking, especially your spouse, stop what you are doing to listen intently, even though you know the matter can wait. It will save you time and improve your relationship in the long run if you do.

The best approach is to write out your arguments. Make sure you have covered every point of everyone concerned. Deliver your thoughts verbally. Be prepared for unexpected reactions or new information so you can fix your arguments "on the fly" (see Topic C-11 at GetLifeRight.com).

Usually, phrases like "I'm not sure," "What do you think?" or "You are right" will win you more friends than being right.

Never speak poorly of a spouse in front of others, even if everyone else is spouse-bashing. That's often the best time to mention some of your spouse's good points.

Deal with the failures of others graciously. People will attempt bigger and better challenges if you react to their failures with understanding and encouragement rather than cautions, criticisms and "I told you so."

> *The easiest way to get things to change is to change the way you look at them.*
>
> —BYRON KATIE

ASK YOURSELF

Which of the basics do I have the most trouble with?

What do I do or say that I can fix on the fly?

SERIES F: Topic 2

Clarifying Your Feelings

When things aren't going right, you tend to look for complicated answers. But the answers are usually simple: Soften your tone, reduce your intensity, get rid of the anger and posturing, stop criticizing and refresh your relationship. One issue that is harder to see has to do with significance. If your work, hobby, commitments or other interests grow, the time you put into them comes from time you could have spent with your spouse. That makes your spouse less significant to you. If your spouse doesn't get a great deal of satisfaction out of what you are passionate about, you are at risk for letting your relationship go flat.

Statements that begin with "I" are clear. Statements that begin with "You" are either criticisms or riddles. Most people would rather help you with a demanding request than try to solve the riddle of why you are angry or what you want.

Examples

"I need you to pay attention to my feelings" is more effective than "You are self-centered."

"I don't deserve your anger" is more productive than "You are short-tempered."

"I would like to see *Titanic* with you next Wednesday night" will get you to more movies than "You never take me anywhere."

"I need you to be more affectionate" communicates desire. A question like "Why won't you make time for us?" is a criticism. It asks the other person to come up with a reason. He knows that anything he says will sound insincere, even if it is honest.

"Would you go to Target with me tomorrow afternoon?" is more likely to get your spouse shopping than "You never go shopping with me."

When you blow up, you often:

- Make a fool of yourself.
- Choose words that don't convey your meaning.
- Lack important facts that could clarify the matter peacefully.
- Damage someone's sense of well being.

Admit your mistakes early and thoroughly. If you've earned the criticism, apologize. Don't make excuses for bad behavior you may have displayed. Be prepared to apologize more than once or in a couple of different ways. Let your actions show you are attempting to make amends.

A spouse who comes home and yells at the kids for leaving toys out on the driveway may be reacting to getting chewed out at work. Instead of responding emotionally, think like a detective. Look for the underlying problem. Handled properly, an "unloading" can be an opportunity to solve a larger problem that has been affecting your relationship on many other levels.

Communication Guidelines

Sound like a friend. Whether you are right or wrong, your tone of voice can create resistance to your words.

Let the "unloader" restate his points (as if his original intentions were incorrectly stated).

Restate the person's position or ask for clarification, e.g., "What you are saying is...?"

Attempt to come up with a complete solution so no part of the issue lingers.

It is always better to own up to your part of a problem, even if your part is very small, than to defend or explain away your position.

Don't try to get the other person to admit his contribution to the blow-up.

Show how you and the other person have the same objectives.

Allow for the fact that the emotions released and words used probably weren't the emotions and words intended by you or the other person.

If your "unloader" wants to make amends by doing something nice for you, let him. Be lighthearted with him while he does so, and show he is forgiven by returning a kindness or doing something cheerful.

When the other person is blowing off steam, let him know you understand the pressures he is under and don't take his outburst personally.

Making up quickly actually strengthens relationships.

Ambition is not a virtue. It does not take precedence over your relationships.

If you can't find a solution to the problem in your relationship, rethink some or all aspects of it as if:

- You are now and are usually overly defensive.
- You are the problem.
- You have misunderstood some facts.
- You have misunderstood the other person's thoughts or intentions.
- You have been acting as if you know the other person's motivations and you don't like them.

As you get better at diagnosing your present problems, you will get better at preventing future problems.

ASK YOURSELF

Do I value the person I am having problems with enough to actually work on my faults?

Is my unwillingness to listen carefully or work on the issues raised, my way of punishing him or her for not listening to me or working on the issues I raise?

SERIES F: Topic 3

Relationship Clues and Cures

When both people in a relationship value each other, it is often easier to fix a problem than most people realize.

You can make up your mind not to be at odds with anyone, and to use your best efforts to defuse any bad feelings that seem to arise.

Turning a Critic into a Friend

How you deal with criticism (or advice) creates many opportunities for bad feelings. No matter how a criticism is made or intended, you get to choose how you receive it. If you counter-punch, you just escalate and perpetuate bad feelings. If you become defensive, exaggerate it or get hurt or super-sensitive, you start to build walls.

Even when the other person's tone or tirade is unwarranted and unacceptable, treat their point as information and disregard the rest. From there, you can say "Thank you, I'll consider it," and then let it go or respond at a better time. Look for ways you can thank the person for his or her thought. It is the easiest way to diffuse the emotions. When you don't take things personally, it can often improve communications.

Before you respond to anyone on any sensitive issue, rehearse your lines in your head. While doing so, look at everything you are thinking of saying from the other person's perspective. Try to find ways to restate the points you want to make so they are less likely to be taken the wrong way.

Here are three of the most common ways you can hurt a person repeatedly (usually your spouse) without being aware you are doing it:

> **Significance**—you keep your interests or activities ahead of your spouse's.

> **Expectations**—you keep your spouse in constant disapproval. It's unhealthy and takes the fun out of life. Could you be asking your spouse to be more than she is by showing disappointment because of something she can't do or can't do as well as you would like?

> **Resentment**—if you have unresolved issues, or have become unwilling to listen or work to compromise on issues that are troubling you, you are probably harboring resentment. If you find criticism in every suggestion, idea or comment, or fail to accept praise or humor, you may be settling for the payoff of being angry and feeling superior. You are choosing the feeling of being right over the closeness you could have.

To change your relationship, change the way you think about it:

- I am willing to look at my own behavior from your point of view.
- If you'll listen with an open mind, I'll tell you what I really think.

- I could be the one who is causing the problems.
- I will stop judging and assigning blame.
- I will listen more completely.
- I will work harder to resolve the problem instead of winning my point.
- I am willing to let go of my resentment before you let go of yours.
- I am willing to go more than halfway to resolve our differences.

A problem well stated is half solved.
−CHARLES KETTERING

Check the box of the habits you have:

☐ Intentionally punish, control, or diminish the other person by not listening adequately.

☐ Allow yourself to have flare-ups often. You may have an exaggerated sense of your own importance and you are using that behavior to intimidate others, to get your way or to keep from having to listen or having to explain yourself.

☐ Be rigid or secretive to hide something you know is wrong that you have already done or want to do.

☐ Have overly sensitive emotional buttons.

☐ Give someone the power to make you overreact and thereby look foolish.

☐ Use a tone of voice or volume that misstates your true feelings.

☐ Present your arguments forcefully, but don't want others to match your intensity with their responses.

☐ Try too hard to hide or minimize your part of the problem.

- ☐ Use words or actions that diminish the other person's efforts or feelings.
- ☐ "Tell on your spouse" or reveal any personal, negative or sensitive matters about your spouse to others, especially in public.
- ☐ Act as if you are responsible for the actions of others, on matters that are none of your business.
- ☐ Admit you have been wrong.
- ☐ Allow too many things to be too important to you.
- ☐ Try too hard to "sell" the points you are trying to make.
- ☐ Make your happiness dependent on another person's being different from whom he or she is?
- ☐ React to everyday problems as if it were a matter of life or death.
- ☐ Keep issues alive by being unwilling to listen to the other person's thoughts, or by not accepting an apology.
- ☐ Hold on to hurts so you can punish the other person by reminding him of his mistakes.

The Reality

When you can't seem to fix the problem, it's usually because you are the problem. You are the only ingredient that is common to all of your problems. Assuming you are to blame, look at what the other person would have been coping with. After your eyes have been opened, use all the honesty you can muster to look at where you have been placing the blame, and look at the logical consequences of those positions.

> **Blame:** My wife doesn't show any interest in what I am doing.

Reality: When I have my "work face" on, I'm touchy and unpleasant.

Blame: My husband never makes time for me anymore.

Reality: I whine and complain, I'm stern, I don't plan, and I'm not fun or affectionate.

Blame: He shows favoritism toward his natural children.

Reality: I won't let him discipline my kids.

Blame: My daughter acts out all the time.

Reality: Nothing she does causes me to listen better, spend more quality time with her, or show her how important she is to me.

Thoughts for Rebuilding Closeness

Rather than tell you what I am not getting out of our relationship, I will tell you what I need.

I'll find ways to make you feel more important to me.

I will acknowledge I could be the cause of the problem or contributing to it.

How I think and feel about an issue causes me more pain than the issue itself.

If a room full of strangers heard the assumptions, explanations and feelings I used to justify my position, would they cheer or boo?

I will praise you for the good you do every day.

I will assume your excited tones are due to pressures elsewhere in your life before I assume you are directing them at me personally.

I will try harder to accept or implement your ideas; will you do the same for me?

Start Your Conversation on the Right Foot

Go to where the other person is before you start talking. Make sure:

- He can hear you.
- She isn't talking on the phone to someone else.
- You are not interrupting her; she could be trying to hold a critical piece of information in her mind in that moment.
- When he can't address the question you raise because he is processing something crucial in his mind, you give him a happy sign that you understand he will gladly ask you to repeat the question when he can. (Otherwise, if you show anger, he will avoid you and your question.)
- Your tone isn't asking her to stop everything immediately to answer you.

Try to work out an understanding between you. For example, "I have trouble responding while I'm on the phone or focused on work. If you will put a note in front of me, I will always give you my undivided attention as soon as I can get free and clear my head."

ASK YOURSELF

Which of my words or behaviors hurt the feelings of others most?

Which relationship problem should I work on first?

Which of my behaviors will be the hardest to fix?

Fixing, Resisting and Controlling

The easiest way for parents to fix children is to maintain such a strong relationship with them that they will do what is expected of them out of respect and appreciation for you.

Adults are much harder to fix. Byron Katie's book, *Loving What Is* gives penetrating ways to solve the deepest difficulties in relationships. One of the hardest faults for some people to see or admit to is control: butting into other people's business and telling them how to live. If you have a relationship that is broken, you can be sure much of the problem is coming from the way you are trying to change the other person and the way the other person is trying to resist your changes, or trying to change you.

When you "love what is," it doesn't mean you become permissive, change your beliefs about what is right and wrong or stop wanting what you want; you simply learn to get your way by becoming workable. It means:

- You use more care in explaining the changes you want.
- You allow the other person more latitude in using his own ideas and approaches to problems.
- You let her know you like it when her way turns out to be the better way.
- You don't repeat your wishes over and over.

- You are very reluctant to find fault.

- You keep your tastes, wants and prejudices in balance.

- You reduce the number of items about which you have strong tastes or opinions, and lower the strength of your opinions on those that remain.

- You use care in dealing with the lapses or failures of others.

- You praise the good efforts of all others.

- You hold your disappointment when the other person is slow to start or forgets the tasks you consider more important than his.

- You adjust to the person's shortcomings, ideally without letting them know.

You can always get your way by letting the other person's way become your way.

While you are attempting to fix another person, you are also saying:

- I will be disappointed if you continue to do things your way.

- You are not as capable as I am.

- You don't measure up to my standards.

- You can't do this task adequately without my direction.

- My right to tell you what to do is more important than your right to do things your way.

- Standard Resisting Practices

- When your controlling ways have imposed on another person who has no way to tell you to back off, that person will:

- Use passive aggression (purposefully keeping the fixer from succeeding without its being obvious).
- Use the silent treatment (punishing the fixer by not talking to him to show her anger, defiance, detachment from or reluctance to comply).
- Ask for endless explanations and clarifications designed to taunt the fixer and make him appear weak, ridiculous, inept or powerless.
- Deliberately anger the fixer.
- Deliberately fail at the matters most important to the fixer.
- Withhold love or approval.
- Fail in order to deny the fixer the satisfaction of causing a change.

The harder a fixer tries to get another person to change, the more unwelcome their efforts become!

Getting a Fixer to Stop

Fixers are not likely to stop fixing, so don't count on it. But sometimes their fixing attempts can be minimized by trying to:

- Change yourself.
- Learn the motivation for the point the fixer is trying to make.
- Let the fixer know you have heard and are considering her input.
- Thank her for the advice.
- Deal with just one issue at a time.

- Report how it benefited you if you used her advice.
- Open up instead of closing up.
- Thank the fixer when she listens to your thoughts.
- Change your manner of responding so the fixer can change his manner of insisting.
- Acknowledge the efforts of those who try to fix you, or change in some way, because if you don't, they will try harder.
- Start with "Thank you"; then add something like "I will give it some thought" or "I have heard what you said, and I will work on it."
- Add, on any very sensitive matter, a statement like "I know you took a risk to share that thought with me. I appreciate that effort and I will give it a lot of thought."

Never pass up an opportunity to say "I was wrong" or "You were right."

Some people (children in particular) push back. They push the buttons of the adult who is trying to maintain control of the situation. They make the adults angry or confused, or force the adults to repeat themselves endlessly. By making the fixer appear powerless, the resister controls the process. What could be more entertaining or rewarding for a strong-willed child than to make an adult appear foolish?

When a religious person sees the soul of a friend at risk, the desire to save that person is powerful. When that soul belongs to an adult, it's a lot riskier. Opening the conversation at the wrong time can close that subject matter permanently. It may be better to wait for the right opening. In some cases, about all you can do is to hope your good example will change your friend.

Controlling Is Advanced Fixing

If you are a hard-core controller, you are least likely to see the error of your way because you believe that your motives are so pure.

While some controllers do it to feel their own power, you may control out of love, conscientiousness, anxiety and protectiveness. Your intentions are good, but your actions often become overbearing. That keeps you from getting the affection you expect, and this can lead to resentment and more use of power. In either case, your subjects may be complying, but they will withhold as much of their life from you as possible, and will likely escape or rebel at their earliest opportunity.

When a person you are talking to has a speck of food in his front teeth, it's like the world stops. You can't think of anything else. Your compulsion to fix him is so strong you can't hear a word he is saying.

When you act that way on too many issues:

- You don't see the negative side of what you are doing because your intentions are so pure.
- You could be insistent, intrusive and authoritarian.
- You are pressing your guidance, corrections, *shoulds* and cautions on those unable to get out from under your control.
- You are likely to cause your subject to grow up to be just like you.
- You have appointed yourself the boss, parent or God's messenger, whose job it is to fix as many of us as you can.

- You are unaware when you are being bossy, super-sensitive, self-righteous, pushy, unwilling to listen or unwilling to forgive without conditions.

When you learn to limit your compulsion to control, you will be rewarded with closeness.

Helpful Thoughts for Recovering Controllers

- Everyone loves Bonsai trees, but nobody would want to be one. We all need some selective pruning now and then, but those who can't stop controlling can disfigure a person who would have been more comfortable and beautiful if allowed to grow in his natural form.

- Others are quite capable of finding reasonable solutions to their own problems.

- Those you allow to be wrong, to color outside the lines and to have and manage their own happiness will become more self-assured than you can make them with incessant cautions and corrections.

- Your approval is a carrot, and your control is a stick. No matter how much better your way is than theirs, you'll gain more compliance with a carrot than a stick.

- Controlling isn't the only tool in your shed; learn to use some of the other ones and start feeling the love.

- Controlling is what people do when they don't have a life of their own or haven't learned how to gain compliance with encouragement and relationships.

Create the right environment, and in time most things will fix themselves. A tiny example: When my granddaughters were 4 and 6 years old, they always pushed too hard on my felt pens, blunting their points. When I was a parent, I would have protected the markers. As a grandparent I protected the girls' creativity by saying nothing. Now, at ages 6 and 8, they love to do art projects near me and they are very good. I get to hear what they plan and how they think. They ask for my advice. They take exquisite care of their own marking pencils. The markers they dulled didn't cost much. The joy of their company and their creativity is priceless.

ASK YOURSELF

Whose love has my controlling cost me?

What am I trying to change about him or her?

Who is paying the highest price for my compulsion to fix?

SERIES F: Topic 5

The Secret to Fixing Others

For a person who is already doing his very best, the slightest comment or bit of advice can be devastating. Whether we are dealing with blemishes or profound moral issues, it takes extreme empathy, care and judgment to know when and how to help another person.

Almost everything we say or do can be received by another as the opposite of what was intended. Take the time you need to learn the mental state and thinking of the person you plan to fix before you blurt out your ideas.

> **Your success with others depends on how skillfully you walk the line between delivering approval or disapproval, giving advice or judgment, suggesting or criticizing, enabling or alienating and being helpful or intrusive.**

It is usually best for people to come up with their own solutions rather than to adopt yours. As much as possible, manage your help so the choices made appear to be those of the person you are helping.

OK Chart

If you absolutely have to fix a person, the OK Chart on the next page will show you how.

OK Chart

DIRECTIONS: Grade the person you want to change and yourself. The higher the number, the more the person is better or worse than OK.

The Other Person							QUALITY	You						
<Below	OK	Better>						<Below	OK	Better>				
3	2	1		1	2	3		3	2	1		1	2	3
							Attitude							
							Adventurous							
							Affectionate							
							Angry							
							Appreciative							
							Attractive							
							Carefree							
							Caring							
							Critical							
							Decisive							
							Forgiving							
							Frugal							
							Fun							
							Generous							
							Helpful							
							Imaginative							
							Industrious							
							Intelligent							
							Lazy							
							Listener							
							Neat							
							Open							
							Organized							
							Parenting							
							Planner							
							Provider							
							Religious							
							Romantic							
							Satisfied							
							Selfish							
							Sensitive							
							Striving							
							Thankful							
							Work Habits							

**Here is the OK Secret: Praise their qualities that
are OK or better, and fix your qualities that are
less than OK.**

That's it! You praise the person you are trying to fix for his qualities above the OK line and allow him to work on his qualities that are below OK in his own way and time. Deal with him as if he is doing his best, and if he isn't, he will do his best in time; and whether he does or doesn't, it's his business, not yours. Then you work on your own qualities that are below the OK line.

The qualities you find so annoying in the other person may not be his; they may exist only in reaction to the way you are. If you weren't in the loop, there might be no problem. Dr. Phil always says, "They're doing what they're doing because you're doing what you're doing."

What you do can be causing, allowing or encouraging the behaviors you don't want in others. When you find and fix yours, theirs may just go away. Fix yourself and others will change.

Let Up
- Stop trying to fix the shortcomings of other people.
- Stop reacting as if their behavior will only continue or get worse.

Lighten Up
- Accommodate the other person as often as you can.
- Do some tasks that are normally done by the other person (e.g., bill-paying, cooking, pet care, etc.).
- Let the other person see you working on subjects listed below your own "OK line."

- Compliment the other person on progress on things below her OK line.
- Share more of your thinking and decision-making with the other person and ask for opinions.

Build Up

- Show support and encouragement.
- Be patient.
- Praise the other person's efforts to find his own solutions (even when he isn't successful).
- As much as possible, let people learn coping skills and the consequences of their everyday decisions from the world instead of from you.
- Avoid prodding, cautioning and running interference for others. Don't overreact to situations.
- Present your thoughts as ideas that are open for comments and changes.
- Don't bring up past issues or shortcomings; deal only with the issue at hand.

Fess Up

- Be quick to admit when you are wrong.
- Show pleasure when someone else's way turns out to be better than yours.
- Let someone know when his input is helpful to you; share praise for his ideas.
- Admit it openly when you don't know, aren't sure or need help.

Warm Up

When a person respects your friendship enough, she may:

- Be more willing to see your points.
- Overlook some of your shortcomings.
- Not interpret your feedback as criticism.
- Work on her own faults more.
- Listen more patiently if she disagrees with you.
- Share her needs with you and associate more happiness with you.

Now go back to the OK Chart and praise the other person's behaviors you haven't praised enough. Then start working on your qualities that are below the OK line.

ASK YOURSELF

What would I fix about myself first?

What praise would be the most helpful to the other person?

How has the way I have been, hurt the person I have been trying to fix?

SERIES F: Topic 6

The "Bubble" Concept

**Your best and most endearing quality may be how
graciously you deal with the things you lack.**

Every person possesses certain capabilities and lacks others.
Some see their own faults as blemishes that others see and dislike,
while others concentrate on their pluses and thrive. Wishing you
were different is harmful to you. Wishing someone else were
different is harmful to them.

When you ask someone for something he doesn't have or can't
give you, your requests can quickly turn to criticism. You can't say
"I'd like you to be different" without implying "You aren't acceptable the way you are." The damage you cause by criticism isn't
limited to the subject you criticized; it hurts the entire person.
You don't have to use words to criticize; you can discount a
person by ignoring him or giving him a look of disapproval with
your body language.

**The qualities and skills we don't have and can't get
are like "Bubbles." There is nothing there.**

Do you wish someone else were different? Is he aware of it? Would
it make his life easier if you quit reminding him? If he thought you
accepted his deficits, would he resist you less, like you more, and
possibly even open up to you? What if you could accept yourself

completely and knew others would too? The "Bubble" concept can do these things for you.

When you draw attention to a person's shortcomings (one of their Bubbles) they build walls to protect themselves from you. When you praise a person for their values, what they can do and the way they are and see them as complete, you build bridges of friendship.

Bubbles don't relate to fault or the lack of a quality; they relate to a skill or a capability you or another person doesn't have. One person may never be able to balance a checkbook, keep a tidy house, do yoga, carry a tune, speak in public or tap dance. Another person may never be able to let her hair down, plan a good vacation, cook, paint or fix a car. Those are Bubbles—hollow spaces in a person's makeup. A good example is Swiss cheese. It is no less tasty because it has Bubbles—in fact, the holes give the cheese its unique character. It is the same way with humans. How gracefully we deal with our Bubbles may make us more lovable than our capabilities do.

The best way to have others overlook your Bubbles is to overlook theirs. It makes you want to return the favor when you know a co-worker is covering for your Bubbles, and that it is okay with her.

You can grant a Bubble to anyone on any issue. It says "Your qualities are so desirable that if you have any shortcomings they aren't significant enough to make a difference." There's no limit to the number of Bubbles you can grant.

To love yourself—including your Bubbles—is to love yourself the way you are. One of the best indications of a good marriage is how well both spouses compensate for the Bubbles of their partner (and benefit from their capabilities).

We all have Bubbles; some are more apparent than others. Take for example the business tycoon who is annoyed that his only son has no interest in taking over the family business. Instead, the son wants to be an actor. The son knows he has a Bubble where his business skills should be, and he doesn't want to embarrass his dad. His dad has no clue he himself has a Bubble where his parenting skills should be. He is driven by his ego and need for accomplishment, and he fails to discover his son has a talent for acting.

A person can appear to have a Bubble that doesn't exist:

1. **If he won't try to develop** a skill he already possesses.

2. **If he is convinced** that he doesn't have a skill, even though he does.

3. **If he doesn't try** because he benefits in some way by not trying.

   Bubbles that are imagined can limit a person as completely as any real Bubbles. Even though some of these can be fixed under the right conditions, treat them all as if they are genuine.

If you wonder constantly whether a person could develop a skill and get rid of his Bubble, he will probably be aware of it and remain guarded around you. If you continue to judge him, you lose the benefits of the Bubble concept.

Deficits serve to keep us humble. Our lack of skills in one area causes us to need others who have the skills we lack. You, in turn, can use your skills to fill in for someone else's lack. By sharing strengths and weaknesses, you become stronger as a team than either of you could be individually.

The president of a company can be an exceptional leader, even though he wouldn't be good at any other job in the company. He can hire people who would be better than he is for the skills he needs.

If you've ever worked around someone who seemed perfect, you will know it makes you feel uneasy.

> **Your success is based on how well you find both those who have what you need and those who need what you have.**

When you try to hide your Bubbles or you are defensive about them, others will usually be aware and may become uncomfortable around you.

> **Love is adjusting to or covering for another person's Bubbles without letting him or her know you are doing it.**

We are all flawed so there will always be plenty of needs to go around. It is a lot harder to receive than to give, but give your need graciously. To the right person, your need is a gift and it is essential for them to be fulfilled in life.

Look at yourself as an actor and your neediness as a role in a play you have been asked to star in. Your role is more difficult than the roll of the person who helps you. Handle it well, and you will get more kudos than the person whose role it was to assist you.

ASK YOURSELF

How much more comfortable would I feel around others if I knew others merely look at my deficits as Bubbles?

Who do I need more approval from?

Who needs less disapproval from me?

Whose deficits have I been drawing attention to?

SERIES F: Topic 7

Reducing Conflict

When a person does something that angers you, it is natural to respond forcefully. Whether the cause of the disagreement is fair or unfair, logical or irrational, accidental or intentional or real or perceived, your emotions still need to be dealt with.

> **If your emotions overpower your reason, you can do lasting damage to a relationship.**

Most arguments are caused when one or both of you act or react before you have all the information. An improper reaction can cause a new argument that is even more heated than the first.

Emotions that are too forceful or don't fit the situation are usually driven by stronger, deeper and less obvious factors that may not be related to the cause of the conflict. Internal issues such as bruised egos, envy, grudges, insecurity or resentment from previous arguments that weren't resolved properly could be at work.

External forces like being reprimanded at work, being ostracized by friends or finding a ding in your brand new car can also cause an overreaction to a smaller problem. When a woman threatens her husband with divorce because he forgot their movie date, it's a symptom of something much deeper than the missed date.

Arguments are perpetuated when one or more people in the exchange are more concerned with winning their point or having their way than they are about finding the best solution for the problem. Most of the time, being happy is better than being right.

Most rants are born of frustration and the expectation that you will not hear or work on the other person's need. Try saying something like this: "You've got some important issues. I want to help. Tell me what you want me to do, and I'll work with you on this problem." If you can do this convincingly, it will disarm them. There will be no need for fault finding, defending yourself, diminishing the other person's arguments, or counter-complaining about their contribution to the problem.

Rather than complain, explain. State the problem. Give an example or two that might produce different results, and ask the other person for his ideas. Don't expect an immediate conclusion. Allow the matter to be unsettled for a while—depending on the issue, perhaps from a couple of hours to a couple of weeks.

Components of an Argument

The **posture** is the way an offended person presents himself using his temper, language, attitude or power. It is his negotiating style. People will assume a posture to make arguments as persuasive as possible and to put the opponent on the defensive. Your posture reveals your intention—whether it is to win, punish or intimidate or to improve the situation. Often the person on the receiving side of your posture will know your position better than you will! Keep in mind that the alienation caused by a posture that is too powerful can make the posture ineffective.

The **hurt** is the degree to which the relationship, trust and feelings of the other party have been injured.

The **infraction** is the act that has angered the other person. That person, if very upset, has likely replayed the incident over and over in his mind and may not be receptive to logic or reason.

Approach and Sequence

1. **Never comment on the other person's posturing unless you can compliment it in some way—even if he is acting crazy.** React as if the other person will be fair and work with you toward a reasonable settlement of the issue. Try to get the other person to reveal anything he hasn't already said about the problem or your relationship.

2. **Attend to the hurt.** Make sure the other person knows the issue is small in relation to the importance of the relationship. Convince the injured party you are genuinely sorry and you understand how you may have caused the hurt. Try not to be defensive.

3. **Accept responsibility for your part of the infraction.** Restate the parts of his arguments that have truth. Mention the ways the other party was not at fault (be generous), or how he could have come to the conclusion he did. Ask questions about his points you do not understand or need to know that might make your side of the argument go away.

4. **Be patient.** Try harder to let the other person win. You can often gain more from allowing the other person to win than you can by winning yourself. Settling an argument in a way that is good for both parties can relieve pressure from elsewhere in your relationship, or make it better than before.

Losing Friends and Arguments

Having the following behaviors while arguing convinces the other person you value your posturing more than their friendship. It also shows you are willing to lose the relationship to prove your point:

- Using explanations that are untruthful, insincere or self-serving.
- Using a demeaning tone of voice.
- Attacking—going after a weakness or sensitivity.
- Embarrassing others—revealing faults or secrets of others in public.
- Being egotistical—being arrogant, unforgiving, self-centered, ungrateful or belligerent.
- Exaggerating your hurt—acting as if you are hurt more or more often than appropriate for what you have experienced, showing self-pity, oversensitivity.
- Pretending—faking a hurt to embarrass the other person so he will leave you alone or lessen his expectations that you will comply.
- Unloading—showing resentment from previous issues.

ASK YOURSELF

What is causing the distance between me and him or her?

How can I get the closeness back?

Can I give up my need to win arguments?

SERIES F: Topic 8

Making Your Point

You can save a lot of pain and bruised feelings if you have the proper skills to deal with arguments and conflicts.

> **Your willingness to work through the issues with the person you are trying to convince may be more persuasive than the arguments you present.**

If you can't take anything less than exactly what you want, it can cause the other person to balk, without even hearing you out. In a heated exchange, almost anything you say can aggravate the other person. If things start to get tense, try to back off and rethink your approach.

Rethinking Your Approach

Understatement is usually more persuasive than superlatives, exaggerations or absolute words like "always" and "never," which suggest you are closed-minded.

The stronger you feel about your point, the more your body language will signal "pressure" to the person you are talking to. (Pressure builds resistance to your thoughts.)

Let the other person buy; don't sell your ideas or solutions.

Speak clearly; never bury your point in a question.

Avoid saying anything that suggests you know what the other person is thinking, intending or feeling, or the reasons for his behavior, opinion or resentment.

Don't bring up past issues.

Men usually talk to sell a point; women speak in order to be heard but not for advice.

Don't ask questions that might make the other person feel he has to defend his position. Don't say anything he might think attacks or minimizes his arguments. You might say something like "I can see this matter is very important to you, and I want to give it very careful thought. Would you please explain... ?" Take whatever the person gives you without questioning it. Offer as little of your judgment on the matter as possible until you know how you want to restate your arguments.

Once you have as much information as you can get, write your presentation down, even if you are going to present it verbally. Wait two days, then reread what you have written. Put yourself in the mind of the other person. If you can, have someone else comment on what you have written. Refine and rewrite your ideas. Even your most caring comments may not be completely right for the other person.

There will always be differences between what you say, think, feel and intend, and what any other person hears, thinks, feels and assumes you mean. Expect to have your ideas rejected initially, and don't overreact. The other person may love your idea or compromise once he understands it. If he doesn't get it right away, be careful not to show disappointment. That might turn him off to the entire subject, or draw his attention away from the ideas you are presenting.

Show you have taken the person's feelings into account. Restate the best of his key points before you deliver yours.

> **Don't present your thoughts as proof you are right, or to try to get the other person to agree immediately; instead, present your ideas for consideration.**

A sample beginning for your presentation might be, "I feel there's still a lot I need to know about your thoughts on the subject. I liked your idea about _____. What would you think if we...?" Then state your new position.

Preserving a Friendship

To keep from burning a friendship, ask yourself:

- What do I hope to gain by what I am about to say?
- How can I respond so my proposed solution makes the other person feel like his points are reflected in the solution? (Even better, make him feel like it's his solution.)
- If I win this point at the expense of the other person, will it be worth it, or might it create some fallout in the future?

If you are convinced the other person cannot change and/or that his reaction is likely to be too harsh, try (if practical without alienating him) to improve a single aspect of his behavior, or try to maneuver him to a place where he can see examples of the behavior(s) you'd like from him.

Example: At the funeral, Frank heard his own daughter eulogize all the ways her father-in-law had helped her and how tenderly he had treated her. Frank, on the other hand, had always been exceptionally harsh. When he realized how much better he could have been as a father, Frank left the church in shame. The next day he told his daughter he would change; and he did, completely.

When you have to deal with a person who is particularly difficult to change, wait for the right moment and then state your case in your version of the following words, and in the order shown.

"When you _____, it makes me feel _____ _____."

"I wish you would _____."

When you have tried to make a point to someone who doesn't accept it, find an authoritative source that states your point clearly in as few words as possible. Give a copy of it to the person you are trying to convince. Give him only the article, not the entire page or book. Be sure to include the source of the article (the authority for the fact or opinion). Consider putting it where the other party will find it (with his mail, perhaps). Try not to pressure him into reading it.

ASK YOURSELF

Do I have any unsettled business with anyone?

How would I rebuild that relationship?

How can I win when my spouse is losing?

What argument have I thought I won, only to wish I hadn't?

SERIES F: Topic 9

Peace Process and Bonding

Start with a loving attitude:

> *Conflict in close relationships is not only inevitable,*
> *it's essential. Intimacy connects people who are dif-*
> *ferent in many ways.*
>
> —MARTHA BECK AT MARTHA BECK.COM

When the Other Person Is Mad

If you won every skirmish and always got to do what you wanted and be the way you wanted, your victories would be short lived, compared to being loved genuinely. Be willing to change for no other reason but that he or she is your partner. Your willingness to change can be the most endearing gift you can give and the one that will give you the most pleasure.

Your spouse's happiness is limited by the way you are to him or her and how you function in the world. While she many not be handling you as well as she could, you surely aren't handling her as well as you could. Look past all that and never quit trying to help your spouse have the best life possible, even if your spouse isn't doing the same for you. Tell your spouse your wishes for you both. Ask for your spouse's wishes and how his or her wishes, if granted, would change your lives. Don't make your willingness to change depend on anything your spouse says or does.

The Peace Process

Try to let things settle down before you respond. Then cover these points in this general order:

1. "I can tell by your anger that this point is very important to you."

2. "It took courage for you to bring it up."

3. "I will do everything in my power to help you with this problem (or to change)."

4. "Tell me more about what's bothering you and what you think I can do to help."

5. "It appears as though I chose my words, actions or emotions poorly. I said things that don't reflect my true feelings."

6. "I can see how what I said, did or was doing would have made you mad." Then say, "What you could not have known was…" or "What I thought was…" or "What I had hoped was…"

7. "I can see that if I had stated my position better (or done something differently), the outcome would have been much better for all of us."

8. Most important, apologize—even if it was not your fault. "Please forgive me."

9. End with something like this: "I like it when we can work on solutions together. I hope you always feel free to share any of your concerns with me, anytime."

Setting the Stage

Try to keep things as neutral as possible and back away if your encounter gets too heated. Restate the things you agree on: "You have some good points. I need some time to think about what you've said; can we talk about them this evening?" Then while you are preparing to present your story, review the following points.

1. Stick to the issues at hand. This is not a good time for you to get other things off of your chest.

2. When your immediate response to a challenge is to defend yourself, state your case or show your anger, your underlying message is this: "Whatever you just said is not as important as what I am about to say." That almost guarantees your response will be discounted in the same way you have discounted their comments.

3. Proceed as if the other person's anger is only an indicator of the intensity of their emotions and that it is not preplanned or meant to hurt you personally (even if it was).

4. You can reduce the other person's anger by listening carefully every time he or she repeats the things that are making him or her angry.

5. In your response and in your proposed solution, restate as many as possible of the good points the other person has made.

6. Present your ideas for consideration only.

Unspoken Anger Creates Distance

The issue that appears to be causing your distance is usually not the cause, only the trigger. The problem is the hidden anger and frustration that comes from not being heard, understood, or treated fairly. You can get and keep your relationship fresh if you follow the case study of Hal and Sally in the next few pages. Many times you can turn the other person's anger into opportunities to reinforce your relationship.

Fixing and controlling, discussed in Topic F-4 at GetLifeRight. com, can rise to the level of addictions. They are among the most common and troublesome causes of anger in a relationship.

SERIES F: Topic 10

Romance—Dwindling to Vibrant:
Hal and Sally

**If your relationship is in worse shape than Hal &
Sally's, diagnosing your problem still requires the
same steps. It will be harder for either or both of
you to see and admit your absolute truths if your
egos, baggage or selfishness are too deep-seated
or you lack the empathy required.**

Hal and Sally had what appeared to be a good marriage, great
kids, friends, security and adventure. But because they chose
their explanations poorly, they missed a lot of the pleasure they
could have had.

For years Hal's work was so demanding that it left very little time
for Sally. She was an exquisite mom and they both had the same
values, but she wasn't interested in the day-to-day workings
of his business or charitable efforts. He succeeded by problem
solving. She was a stay-at-home mom who looked at his attempts
to change anything as criticism. She was sensitive on other issues.
Her way of looking at them usually cast him as the bad guy. That
reduced the number of topics they could talk about. Over time
she took his quietness as disapproval. She thought his quietness
showed his lack of interest in her. For the things he did right, he
got very little praise.

Eventually Hal adjusted to the way Sally appeared to be by not sharing some of his ideas, by not saying anything that could be construed as criticism, and by adopting the "Loving what is" philosophy (ByronKatie.com). He contented himself with the person and relationship that remained. He presumed she wasn't very affectionate. The thought of being more affectionate or saying, "I wish you were more affectionate" never entered his mind.

With that settled, he gave most of his attention to business and charity work. Sally continued to go without the enthusiastic affection she craved.

None of these conditions were good for their sex life. He knew she wasn't being satisfied, and he had tried everything he had read or heard about to make it better. His performance anxiety was so high that the last thing he wanted was an orgasm because it would mean he had failed again to satisfy her. One night she blew up. She accused him of not caring, being selfish and worse. It seemed to him she wanted to hurt him as much as she possibly could, and hurt him she did. She never apologized. He didn't try to defend himself, tell her he cared or that he didn't deserve that kind of criticism. They just stopped having sex.

If Hal had known the Peace Process (Topic F-9 at GetLifeRight. com), he would have seen Sally's blow-up as a perfect opportunity to reaffirm his love for her and remind her of what a nice man she married. The episode would have cleared the air and brought them closer together than ever. Instead, he reacted to her attack by reducing his interaction with her further. It was the worst decision he had ever made.

In preparing for her funeral two years later, Hal found handwritten notes in Sally's diary and Marriage Encounter booklet. In them, he saw the girl he had married. She was far softer than he realized, and she had suffered more than he knew. He meant more to her than she let on. He absolutely loved the person in her words. She wrote about how important sex was to her and how close it made her feel to him. He cried for days.

The instant Hal read those words he knew he had cheated them both out of the intimacy they could have been having. If she had given him what she had written instead of her wrath, he would have moved heaven and earth to make her happy. She had chosen the wrong explanation to describe her need. He chose the wrong response. After the shock and sadness of her writings on intimacy and several other issues, Hal wanted to know why neither of them had spoken up.

Why didn't he look past what she said and how she said it to find what she needed and how he could have helped?

Martha Beck, a famous life coach, found that many women just don't know how to express their needs. Martha knew that for people to live joyfully, they must learn to open up (MarthaBeck. com). Hal knew there was more than enough love between him and Sally, but neither of them could open up. As a result, they had to settle for good, when a sensational relationship was well within their grasp.

Hal asked several people for input on his story, and all the guys spoke immediately in excited tones. They told him they could never get their wives to tell them what they needed. The guys admitted it was hard for their wives to get their attention, but they would be happy to change if their wives would make a reasonable case, and approach them as friends instead of enemies. Their reaction was comforting, but Hal needed a bigger answer. Hal wanted to know the absolute truth about what happened, and he was prepared to tell the absolute truth about his part.

Hal's Absolutely Truthful Explanations

With the help of his friends who knew Hal and Sally well, Hal explained that:

- Her outburst was an uncontrollable cry for help on a subject she didn't know how to deal with, and he responded to her anger in the worst possible way.

- Most of Sally's emotional wounds were legitimate and inflicted by him.

- His anxious ways were not good for intimacy.

- His preoccupation with goals was all-consuming.

- He had given Sally what he thought was enough time and attention, but it was neither generous nor enough.

- The moment she was gone, he knew he had not celebrated her existence enough.

- Hal thought he had a Bubble where his ability to celebrate life should have been, but he also had to admit he would have done better if he had made it more of a priority.

- Hal got plenty of satisfaction from his work. Sally got no satisfaction from hers because he was her work and he acted too self-sufficient.

- He didn't seek out her company in ways that were satisfying to her.

- He didn't look deeply enough into her needs.

- Even if she was completely wrong, reluctant to change and never sure of what she wanted, she still was worthy of more thought and effort than he had given her.

- Hal opened up more to others than to Sally because he never knew how she would react; his lack of openness made her saddest of all.

- He adjusted to the person he thought she was.

Sally's Absolutely Truthful Explanations

With the help of Sally's writings, Hal and his friends tried to understand what Sally's absolute truth would have been.

- Sally's sensitivity made too many subjects off limits.

- She treated his successes as expected rather than celebrated.

- She dealt with not being loved "the way she wanted to be" by dwelling on her hurts rather than appreciating her blessings and opportunities.

- She never said she was sorry for anything.

- She seemed to have stronger opinions on what to do, so he let her do the planning. She had plenty of time to plan activities, and he would have done anything she asked.

- She didn't want to do all the planning because she wanted to feel taken care of by him, at least some of the time.

- She adjusted to the person she thought Hal was.

- The lack of happiness she projected was a barrier to receiving the type of love she wanted.

- She couldn't find the words; perhaps because *they had never created a forum where all communications were save and cherished.*

> **When you can't find the words or the nerve to bring up an issue, either you don't have a safe place in your marriage or you are unsafe when you talk. Let your spouse or prospective partner know that you want to be safe and that you want a place where all conversation is heard and appreciated.**

Conclusions

"**Loving what is**" about a person helps to reduce your compulsion to change them. While that is generally good advice, it should not be taken as a signal to stop investing in the relationship. Hal and Sally both stopped looking for the relationship that could be.

> **Every marriage is worthy of repeated attempts to achieve "What can be."**

Hal and Sally were both very good people. They both knew they deserved more affection and concern than they were getting. They had let their big issue go so long that new attempts by either of them seemed awkward.

Steps to Closeness

Replace Annoyance with Reassurance

We all have annoying manners. Most of them are low-end communication skills—postures or negotiations used to get your own way without having to justify our position. They show lack of empathy and respect. If you respond to them with your own annoyance, you encourage more. Deal with your spouse's annoyances on your terms later on.

Ask your Annoying Spouse to state in clearer terms what he or she wants or would like to accomplish. Try to limit your discussion to one issue at a time, and concentrate on it. Offer your support and compliance where possible. Don't feel the need for closure. Solutions are easier to agree on after emotions have calmed down.

Being annoying is a choice. Choose to replace your own annoying ways with reassurance and praise before and after every issue. Without using words, your reassurance will say "I am communicating in a loving way, and it would be nice if you did too."

> **Every time you respond to your spouse, you either improve or degrade the environment in which your future thoughts and emotions will be exchanged. The warmth of your responses is the true measure of your love.**

Reset Your Relationship Often

You can put your love first by praising and thanking each other often. Use the Peace Process (page ___) on the substantial issues. Explain yourself more fully so your spouse understands your motivation, intentions and how he or she can help. If you listen well enough, you may find out that you have been discounting your spouse by undermining his or her efforts, or that he or she has a Bubble, has been struggling or needs more approval from you. All of those conditions are reasons to love your spouse more.

Refresh your relationship, and many of the problems you had, or thought you had, will disappear.

Communication

Whenever you feel you and your spouse are not on the same wavelength, reset your relationship. Here are some ideas:

1. "I want you to be as happy as you can be. To do that you need to be able to speak the absolute truth about what you think and feel on any subject. I will do my best to make you feel completely safe with anything you share, including the things that might hurt my feelings."

2. Give her a copy of "A True Friend" (the first bolded idea shown on page 142).

3. "I need some down time with you. If I took you to _____ this weekend, do you think you could tell me what's bugging you about me?"

4. There isn't anything about you that I don't love.

5. "I feel good about us, but I am not sure that you do. Can you tell me what is troubling you?"

6. Try breaking the tension with something silly. "If you don't tell me what's bothering you by the time I count to 5, I am going to tickle you till you fart."

Clumsy words and disjointed ideas are better than making no attempt. If you have to deal with annoying matters, speak kindly of the comments of your Annoying Spouse. Even when you are positive your Annoying Spouse has done something wrong inten-tionally, use the Peace Process.

Findings on Intimacy

Without affection, your love life will deteriorate. Being shy and long suffering hurts you and your partner. No matter how awkward, you owe it to your spouse to speak up. Some women rarely if ever have orgasms. They may give you a pass, but on some level they feel inadequate or unloved when it doesn't happen. A lot of spouses would rather die than tell you how dreadful you are in the sack. If your spouse gives you any hint, no matter how small, take is seriously.

When Hal and his friends asked for input from others, surprisingly two married women volunteered that they hadn't had orgasms in decades. Apparently:

> **Lots of married people are reluctant to tell their spouses that it isn't happening for them.**

Hal had taken a class on reproduction in college and read about it over the years. He was sure he knew the basics and the improvisations and had tried most of them. Without some fertility issue involved, neither he nor Sally would have gone to a sex therapist. He didn't think Sally would respond well if he suggested she do some homework or try some experimentation of her own.

A year after Sally's funeral, Hal was looking for a book title he overheard mentioned in a restaurant. On the subject of female orgasms, Google listed that book along with fourteen million other inquiries or listings on the subject. Without reading a word of the book or any item on the list, he knew in another profound way that he hadn't paid enough attention to Sally's needs. He hadn't done as much for her as he could have, and he knew he would regret it forever.

Sally could have helped herself by being clearer about her needs, yet she may not have even known what those needs were. She also had more free time to solve her problem than Hal did. The same information was there for her to find too. If her thought-energy had been directed toward finding her own solution rather than on the ways Hal was letting her down, she could have helped them both.

Sally did not go looking for solutions to her problem because she had already concluded that Hal would react poorly. She had adjusted to the person she thought Hal was. She had prejudged him.

Hal never approached the subject of sex from the standpoint of needing it. He thought about it a lot and tried his best, but he never really let her know how important it would be for him to be able to satisfy her. When he gave up, he never tried to compensate by cuddling more.

Hal never approached the subject of sex from the standpoint of needing it, but he also never told Sally how important it would be for him to be able to give her pleasure.

Having some abandon helps. If your problem can't be solved, have an understanding something like the one that follows:

- ☑ Be lighthearted.
- ☑ If you coach me, I will listen and do my best.
- ☑ I will work with you, read up, or seek help.
- ☑ If that doesn't work, I'm sure we can find ways to have more fun trying.
- ☑ All we need is a little more practice.

☑ Your affection and happiness are the most important things to me.*

☑ For solutions you try to implement, you must have the best interests of your partner at heart. Ideally you will feel close enough to share each other's absolute truths. With issues like infidelity, ego, baggage, selfishness, self-contentment, insecurity, control, inferiority or addiction, you will have to fix yourself before the changes you agree to can be relied upon; and that could take a long time.

SERIES F: Topic 11

Refreshing Your Relationship

Sally had grown weary of trying to fix her relationship. She believed Hal was too set in his ways; and since she had tried everything, she adjusted to the person she thought he was. To Sally, almost everything he did seemed to be more important to him than she was, and everything he said was an attempt to fix her. The monthly relationship books she read offered her a few vague suggestions but they also pointed to new ways to see how Hal was disappointing her.

In Sally's efforts to change Hal, he had no idea how strongly she felt or what he could have done to satisfy her. That there was something wrong with him was implied in everything she said to him. She assumed nothing she said registered with Hal. But he remembered everything; including how good it felt on the day she took his hand while they were walking in public a long time ago.

To the world, Sally was sweetness and light; to Hal, she had become detached. That distance guaranteed she would not get the affection and attention she wanted. She acted as if her affection were something to be given, but only after all the fixing is done.

Sally wasn't weary, she was disheartened. She would have had unlimited energy if she thought she could change Hal. If she had changed the way she thought, or the way she responded to him, the problem might have solved itself. Hal didn't need fixing; he just needed appreciation, affection, and reasonable requests, stated as if she knew he loved her and wanted what was best for her.

Hal wasn't aware of when or if Sally had given up on him, because he had already adjusted to Annoying Sally (the person she seemed to be). Hal could live with her the way she was being. Almost every day he would ask her, "Is there anything you would like to do today?" Her answer was always "No." He could never figure that out.

> **Affection was Sally's trump card, but she held it back. Maybe she thought she would use it once she fixed Hal; maybe she was on autopilot or had no affection to give.**

A Prescription for Your Marriage?

Getting your closeness back may be difficult at first, but here are some of the best ideas:

- Show as much affection as possible.
- Be sure to touch your mate every chance you get.
- State your needs without criticism or sarcasm; making him feel worse about himself is not a good way to make him feel better about you.
- Show interest in what she is doing or likes to do.
- Watch him work if he will let you, and be his best fan.
- Use "I" statements: "I need you to help me pick out a lamp," not "You never take me shopping."

- Use praise before and after your requests.

- Let her know you are giving a lot of thought to the things she suggests, and agree with her as much as you can.

- Bring out and share your pictures and recollections about the time when you were first dating or married.

- Speak to your partner as if you fully expect him or her to respond openly and with your best interests at heart.

- When your spouse asks what you'd like to do, *want* to do something. If you do not, your burden your spouse with the responsibility of making the decisions, organizing the event and entertaining you.

This process could take a while, but once he gets the idea he will try to pay you back. He may even try to "out-nice" you. This is the surest way to get the most out of your spouse. With the slightest encouragement, you both could be like school kids with crushes.

The walls between you aren't from lack of interest; they are from the way you have been reacting to each other. What has been making you weary is not your expenditure of energy; it's the feeling that nothing you do will work, or that you aren't willing to take any more emotional beatings because your spouse's responses have hurt you so deeply and so often. The thought of making your spouse happy when you aren't seems so overwhelmingly unfair that you aren't going to budge. Bear in mind that when a person quits trying, she could be putting on a pout or a negotiation or getting an emotional payoff from feeling righteous about her position. Your own pride is the first place to look and the easiest thing to change, if you are willing to.

Perks

To keep your relationship fresh, pour on the perks. Perks are rewards or advantages we give that show the recipient he or she is special. The thought behind a well-selected perk is usually more significant than the size of the perk. A flower on a pillow or washing her car might make your girl feel special. Do you give your spouse enough perks? Which of these broad categories would mean more to your spouse?

> **Time**—doing the things with her that she likes best.
>
> **Gifts**—with sentimental value that are appropriate or unexpected.
>
> **Tasks**—doing things that are normally her responsibility.
>
> **Affection**—verbal and physical.
>
> **Praise**—especially in front of others.

If you were dating, you'd be creative in finding interesting ways to entertain and enjoy your date. If you aren't just as imaginative for your spouse, you are probably letting your marriage go flat. Set up a date night every other week. Make it a priority to celebrate each other's existence and refresh your relationship. (Avoid the temptation to discuss how expensive your meal is.)

Refreshing Ideas

Refresh your marriage to keep it genuine and natural in all things.

Celebrate the existence of your spouse in every way you can.

Expressing affection, empathy and good listening skills are the best ways to get the closeness you want.

Inside the person you are having issues with now is the one who dazzled you when you first met. Find the first pictures of you together, frame them, and hang them around the house. They will make you fall in love over and over again. Your spouse will feel cherished. It will be good for your kids to see how you honor each other.

"Hon, I'm feeling uncomfortable; is there anything about me or us that is bothering you?"

"You are my best friend. I like everything about you. It may be hard for you to get my attention, but I want everything about us to be as good as we can get it."

Showing support for the things that interest your spouse will get you more affection than managing the house and kids flawlessly or bringing home the largest paycheck.

Pursue interests of your own so you can bring fresh experiences to the family and assume more responsibility for your own happiness.

Develop your own capabilities, strengths and interests. They give your spouse opportunities to talk about what you like and pay you back for the support you give him or her.

Showing interest in what your mate does will get you more affection than reminding him or her of the ways he has disappointed you.

Making her feel loved is a good way to get her to see your side of an issue.

Asking her to change in ways that conflict with the core of her being and beliefs is not a good way to show love.

Most people like activities that are familiar, unfamiliar, peaceful, and exciting; plan some of each for your spouse.

Do some of the chores on your spouse's responsibility list. Watch the kids to give your spouse more personal time. Bring him or her coffee in the morning. Fill her car up with gas.

Be fun.

Cook or help to cook a meal.

Stay by her side while she is shopping and push the cart.

Brainstorm the direction of your lives and freshen up your goals, especially the non-business aspects of your marriage.

Renowned author and speaker Christiane Northrup, MD, said something to the effect that, "There is nothing more exciting than to have a new partner." She also said, "You can become that new partner over and over by bringing new experiences to the relationship."

Find and share ideas on how to refresh your relationship at GetLifeRight.com/Refresh.

ASK YOURSELF

How can I make him or her feel special?

How can I give more affection?

Create and Maintain a Close Family

Be the glue that holds these
irreplaceable parts together.

SERIES G: Topic 1

Dating

Dating is exciting because to make a good connection you have to make yourself vulnerable. It is extremely satisfying when you find a relationship that brings out your best qualities. There is nothing more exhilarating than a close encounter with a person who could be the right match for you. The person you are dating could put you in touch with, and appear to be, the answer to some of your most profound emotional needs. He or she could give you validation and make you feel more alive than you have ever felt.

Many people are more afraid of dating than of speaking in public. Dating causes you to reveal yourself and risk that some of your weak parts might be found unacceptable. When you are comfortable with yourself, it makes others feel relaxed around you. If your relationship continues, the other person will eventually find out what you are like, so resist the temptation to appear different than you really are. For many people the best single piece of advice is:

Making your relationship work before you marry is the best way to know how it will work once you're married.

Having a teammate—someone you can speak to openly and comfortably on any subject—is the most romantic and endearing experience you can have. It is sharing the same goals, covering for each other, and "pulling on the rope in the same direction."

It often takes more than a year for a candidate to feel comfortable enough around you for you to observe his or her less desirable traits. You won't find a cockroach every time you turn on the light, but when you find one, there could be many more nearby. Take as much time as you need to make sure you know what you are getting.

Dating is the audition during which you both gather the information you will need to render a good decision. Know your partner's thinking, attitudes and beliefs on every subject, and make sure he or she has the same information about you. You both need to try to avoid making a mistake.

Go for the quality, be patient and look for the land mines before you sign up. (Yes, there will be land mines.) Your marriage, no matter how well you have chosen, will present you with the biggest challenges of your life. Those challenges will keep you humble and flexible, but also happy—if you both have the right qualities and attitudes.

You are getting your candidate "as is." If you feel you need to change him or her, you will be in for a lifetime of aggravation and disapproval (see Topics F-4, Fixing and Resisting, and F-6, "Bubbles," at GetLifeRight.com).

It is better if the skills, deficits and qualities of the other person dovetail with yours. While opposites have produced many of the best marriages, those marriages are riskier. When in doubt, do more homework.

The characteristic that once made your spouse so appealing can drive you crazy over time.

- The big spender may keep the family finances shaky your entire life together.

- The "looker" who primps for hours may make you late for every event.

- A messy house may be the price for her hobby or carefree spirit.

- The handsome guy who needs everything his way will get uglier.

- The wonderful provider has no time for you or the kids.

- The wife who loves to cook may make you heavier than you should be.

- Know and like the family of your candidate; someday they may need to move in with you or you with them. Over time, more of their characteristics will be visible in your spouse.

Treat every date as a rehearsal for the date that follows.

Finding dates—go where the guys/girls are, or where you can find people who do what you enjoy. Reduce the time you spend on solitary interests like reading or surfing the Web. Get a job where you can interact with people of the opposite sex. Tell your friends and acquaintances you are interested in meeting a quality person.

Internet—let your computer expand your market and do some prescreening for you. Some of the online dating services include spark®.com, eHarmony®.com, Match.com®, Christian-Mingle. com®, SpeedDate.com™, It'sJustLunch.com® or, for people over 50, OurTime.com. Costs for these services at the time of this writing range from $25 to $60 per month. Features and privacy issues of these services vary widely, so check them out before you commit. Some people have made connections through Craigslist. org (which are classified ads on the Internet).

Arrange to meet in a neutral public place until you are comfortable revealing where you live. Create and use a secondary email address for screening candidates.

Nothing can validate or fulfill a person more than the right person. But romance is art—and there is no accounting for taste. The other person gets to cast the only vote and can have a change of mind any time. If there's no magic, you can't manufacture it.

Stress-Busting Hints

- Be the first person to attempt to get acquainted.
- Remember that her topics are more interesting to her than your topics are.
- Nice comments about her appearance show you appreciate her effort to look good for you. Showing interest in her life, thoughts and interests suggests your interest in her is genuine. Comments about her physical characteristics can suggest you are shallow and that her looks are more important to you than her substance.
- Accept your date the way he is.
- Practice your social skills with everyone you meet.
- Questions about her youth, family, and where she grew up are usually good conversation starters.
- Before asking for a date, give her some details on what you propose to do. If you give her a choice, give her details on both.
- Start with a low-key outing such as a bike ride, hike or public event. Select a quiet location where you can hear each other and where your date will feel safe so you can talk easily.
- Have your cell phone turned off.
- Remember, you don't learn unless you listen.

- Don't panic if conversation lags; remember, this experience is a trial run. Your date may be shy or lack conversation skills, too—relax.

- Keep two or three questions or topics in mind to talk about in case you have to jump-start the conversation. Be slow to move from one topic to the next.

- Give the other person enough information about your interests to help him or her to form questions about yours. Be careful not to let talk about your interests use up all the time or trump the other person's interests.

No matter how close you seem to have grown in any encounter, unless the person is willing to accept you and all your Bubbles you don't have a connection. When the relationship goes away, losing the conditions that validated you is more serious than losing the person. Your need caused you to see more in the relationship than was actually there. Appreciate the moments together and use the lessons you learned to improve your skills for your next relationship. Chasing a romance rarely works. It tends to make you annoying, and you will probably end up embarrassing yourself in the process.

There is no such thing as being rejected, only not being chosen.

Once your interest has been rejected, let it go. You were fortunate to have the practice and the memories. The song "Haven't Met You Yet" by Michael Bublé can get you in the right frame of mind for the search.

ASK YOURSELF

What can I work on to help me become the right person for the type of person I want to marry?

What do I like doing?

I know I'm the bait and I have to put myself where the fish are. Where am I most likely to find a good candidate and have enough time with her to get acquainted?

Where could I find candidates who are doing things I would like to do?

SERIES G: Topic 2

Look Before You Leap

Over half of all marriages in the U.S. fail; learn the risks and do your homework. Falling in love can make you feel better than you have ever felt, but people get blindsided when they let that euphoria prevent them from learning about their partner.

Take as much time as you need to observe your relationship objectively. Ask trusted friends and family for their honest input, and listen to it: In California, for example, an "ex" can get half of everything you own in a one-time payment up front, plus alimony after that. Those with kids could have to pay 40% of their net income for the next 18 years and maybe help with medical costs, day care, private school and college tuition—and still have to pay the taxes on all the money before their spouse gets his or her allotment.

Make sure the person you are about to marry will be reasonable, ethical, and principled—even through a heated divorce (and until your last child turns 18).

The parent who retains custody of the kids becomes their gate-keeper. A vindictive or unforgiving person can restrict your access to the kids until they are 18, inflict great emotional pain on your children, and suck up any money you might have had left to share with a new partner who loves you.

Watch how your candidate handles problems or conflicts with other people, especially if he or she has been wronged. With whom and with what kind of people and what kind of issues does he or she have problems now?

It is unrealistic to assume you can fix anything about the person. Your candidate's deficits or Bubbles are part of the deal. You owe it to your candidate to reveal your own faults and deficits as well. A marriage may solve a problem or "balance" you two out, but never count on it.

The drive of your prospective spouse is a major issue overlooked by many people who are dating. When spouses share a cause— which could be a worldly ambition (to get rich) or a spiritual one (to do good)—life is good. All success requires a great deal of emotional commitment over a long time. If one person is driven by a cause and the other isn't, eventually the one who isn't has to compete with the cause for attention.

You also owe it to your prospective spouse to have some interests of your own. If you have none, you burden your spouse with the responsibility of making you whole when you haven't been able to do that yourself.

> **When you can talk to your prospective spouse openly about anything, you are on your way to a good marriage. But even couples with good communication skills have to work hard at their relationship.**

The following list points out some of the critical areas where you and your potential spouse need agreement or understanding. If you don't have the courage to get into each one of these subjects, you could be courting disaster.

You need to know:

- Philosophy and strength of convictions regarding politics and religion
- Life goals and purpose
- Values and morals (past and present)
- Ties and relationships with parents and family
- Specific plans about starting a family (number of kids and time-line desired)
- Parenting skills and philosophy
- Views on day care vs. full-time parenting
- Drive for personal development, growth and accomplishment
- Current debt and responsibility with money
- Coping skills; how each handles crises
- The way he or she fights and makes up
- Willingness to forgive
- Track record of quitting or persisting
- Perceived roles for each spouse
- Types of friends and influences
- Medical issues, addictions and/or conditions
- Commitment to health
- Views on charity and "giving back"
- Preferred recreation (active or inactive)
- Attitudes/expectations about sex
- Desired places to live (when, where and why)
- Dependencies (family medical histories)

Even when you have done your homework you will still have plenty of challenges. Your candidate can change her mind at any time about any issue. Since your candidate's family comes with the package, find out what they're like. Caution: Those who remarry tend to marry people with the same traits as their ex. Look for signs. If you fit into that mold, you could be on your way to becoming his or her next "ex."

Like a drug, sex clouds people's judgment. It's like having a third entity in your relationship that is powerful, selfish and greedy and only cares about one thing. The person you are dating can be more in love with that entity than you. The earlier you give yourself away sexually, the harder it is to know the qualities of the person you are dealing with. If you hope sex will be enough to sell the rest of you, you can be sure it will—until he or she finds a more attractive donor. With the prevalence of sexually transmitted diseases, you are taking enormous risks: One mistake and you could harm your sex life with the person you marry. Why play Russian roulette? The fallout of an unwanted pregnancy can be devastating to you, your child to be and your career. Children deserve and need two parents.

ASK YOURSELF

Do I trust him or her enough to work through this list?

What will half of my net worth be 10 years from now?

Is he or she reluctant or cooperative? Is he or she looking for alternatives, or wanting to change the subject?

SERIES G: Topic 3

Compatibility Checklists

Above all, marriage is communication. Every item on these lists provides a window into how well you will be able to communicate as a couple.

If these issues are difficult for you, or you can't talk about them now, you aren't ready to take the plunge. Make two copies of these lists, one for each of you. Give your real answers (not the ones you think the other person wants to hear). Address your fears or live with them. The subjects you need your candidate's thoughts on most will be the hardest for you to ask about. Most people will not know their true thinking on some issues. If you are unsure about his or her answers to important questions, ask your questions at different times in other ways.

Subjects for agreement :

- On important decisions, no action can be taken until we both agree.
- Any subject can come up for reconsideration at any time, and as often as necessary, until an agreement is reached.
- Unless there is disagreement on a subject, we will generally let the person who cares the most or is the most knowledgeable about the subject make the call.
- We will always act in the best interests of the family.

- We each agree to take responsibility for our own happiness.
- I will be more valuable to you if I also value myself.
- I will be kind, open and honest about how I feel.
- I will not badmouth you in front of the kids or in public.
- I will try my best and believe you will, too.
- I want you to feel you can always lean on me when you need help.
- I promise to take your preferences into consideration while channel surfing.

When pouring out your hearts on a concern, she usually wants you to listen and comfort her, whereas he wants to give or get advice. Let your spouse know how you like to be heard most of the time.

When you complete the form on the next two pages, then ...

ASK YOURSELF

Which question was I most afraid to ask?

Which answer made me proudest of my candidate?

Which ones do I need to check out further?

Compatibility Checklist

His present total debt is $ _____

   and consists of   _____

Her present total debt is $ _____

   and consists of   _____

1. I think we should limit our credit card debt to _____

2. He wants _____ Boys _____ Girls

3. She wants _____ Boys _____ Girls

4. Let's begin having kids when?   He: _____

                                       She: _____

5. I believe parenting is the primary responsibility of:

   He says: Husband ____ % Wife ____ % Both ____ %

   She says: Husband ____ % Wife ____ % Both ____ %

6. His primary parenting style is more: ☐ Permissive ☐ Strict

7. Her primary parenting style is more: ☐ Permissive ☐ Strict

8. He wants her to be an "at home" mom   ☐ Yes   ☐ No

9. She wants to be an "at home" mom   ☐ Yes   ☐ No

10. She wants to work outside the home starting when the
    youngest child is what age? _____

11. My idea of a good vacation is to _____

    _____

12. The bank account should be the responsibility of   ☐ Him ☐ Her

13. Access to our bank accounts should be by, she says: ☐ Him ☐ Her

                                          he says: ☐ Him ☐ Her

14. I feel strongly that I should control the following matters:

    _____

Checklist, continued

15. Rate the following items in their order of importance to you:
    (1 being most important, 5 being least important)

    _____ **Friendships**   _____ **Family tradition**   _____ **Faith**

    _____ **Comfort**   _____ **Education**

16. He wants to save/invest, starting: ☐ Now   ☐ 1 yr   ☐ 5 yrs

17. She wants to save/invest, starting: ☐ Now   ☐ 1 yr   ☐ 5 yrs

18. He thinks we should save: $ _____ per _____

19. She thinks we should save: $ _____ per _____

20. In each of the following areas, whose taste should be favored?

    Décor: ☐ **Him**   ☐ **Her**   ☐ **Both**

    Yard: ☐ **Him**   ☐ **Her**   ☐ **Both**

    Garage: ☐ **Him**   ☐ **Her**   ☐ **Both**

21. Tidiness is: ☐ not important ☐ somewhat important ☐ a big deal

22. My faith life is:

    ☐ not important to me   ☐ somewhat important   ☐ very important

23. Divorce is acceptable only under the following circumstances:
    She believes _____

    _____

    He believes _____

    _____

24. In the event of divorce, I believe any assets and liabilities I bring to the marriage should be returned to me.

His answer _____   Her answer _____

25. The assets and liabilities we have accumulated together should be divided equally.

His answer _____   Her answer _____

SERIES G: Topic 4

Marriage

Your Marriage Is the Home of Your Relationship

Marriage subjects our happiness to the whims, moods and inadequacies of another person. We all have powerful and specific feelings about almost every issue. We all have weaknesses and faults, so finding a person who is "workable" is crucial. Workability can only be determined by talking openly about a lot of subjects over time. Take your time; get it right.

> **Many times one or both people project their wants and needs onto the person they are about to marry, and then marry that image instead of that person.**

That sets up one or both parties for disappointment because it's the reality you will have to live with for your entire marriage.

It may seem like the easy way out is to divorce, but statistics tell us we tend to make the same mistakes going forward. Each successive marriage has a higher rate of failure than the one before it.

> **Many of those who have been married multiple times admit the compromises they had to make with subsequent spouses were just as great as the ones they chose not to make to save their first marriage.**

They felt that, overall, their first spouse was just as good as or better than subsequent spouses.

My responsibilities 📩 :

- To take responsibility for my own happiness.
- To work on my limitations diligently.
- To compromise willingly.
- To be able to financially support the family if necessary.
- To stop what I am doing and listen attentively when my spouse is talking.
- To accept his or her Bubbles cheerfully.
- To readily admit when I am wrong.
- To be offended less and be more open about my feelings.
- To show faith and support for my spouse.
- To get over my hang-ups, baggage, sarcasm and attitude.

It's Never Too Late to Give Up

Fred's marriage had never been very good. Anita refused to understand his side of any issue and interpreted his comments as criticism. In about their 30th year of marriage he finally realized what he was doing wasn't working. He gave up and quit wishing she were different. That made her less defensive, and they both started to notice some of the qualities that attracted them to each other in the first place. Today they are enjoying life and each other more than ever.

ASK YOURSELF

What am I doing to annoy my spouse?

What have I gained from being that way?

How can I nag less and show more affection?

SERIES G: Topic 5

Parenting

A child's primary drive is to achieve a place of importance in the family structure and gain the attention that goes along with it. If he can't earn it by constructive means, he will take it any way he can get it. This need can be so great in some children that they will take it in ways that are harmful to him and the family.

Your most powerful asset is the relationship you have with your child. Relationships are more important than issues. Children will often do more for those with whom they have a close relation-ship than they would for themselves.

The time between birth and 3 years of age is when children need their parents the most because that's when their programming is being established. That's when they form their opinion of how helpful or frightening the world is.

> **Children, especially young ones, need the "Three P's"—potency, permission and protection.**

> **Children who are listened to and whose opinions are valued tend to live with the assumption that the world will also treat them this way.**

Parents who do too much for their kids teach their children that other people exist to wait on them. This unrealistic expectation prevents children from developing their own coping skills or taking responsibility for their actions. It sets them up for prob-lems in relating to others for years to come.

It is not good for one child to be compared to another, no matter how good a point you think it will make. You could alienate them to each other, and that's bad for both of them.

Parents of well-behaved children avoid parents whose kids are troublemakers. Well-mannered kids also stay away from disobe-dient children. Your child's misbehavior limits his choices of friends to other kids with behavior problems. As your child ages, he faces more and more peer pressure. By his teenage years, you will be competing with his peers and the media for his attention; and unless your child has a strong self-image, he will likely be persuaded by his closest pals to do things he shouldn't do.

Your children's choices in the future will depend on how well you have been able get them into interesting and wholesome activi-ties. The following is a list of some of the best ideas for developing their judgment, confidence, persistence and sense of significance:

- Have fun with them.
- Expose them to sources of inspiration.
- Take them on outings where they can see the results of others who have succeeded in doing what they are about to do.
- Describe several ways to look at various things that are happening and the most logical outcomes for each course of action, and encourage them to do the same.
- Let them see they can influence you with their good ideas.
- Show them you are just as interested in helping them enjoy life as you are in helping them assume responsibility.
- Explain to them the purpose of what you do and what you want them to do.

- Keep them away from people, experiences or media that could cause them to grow up too soon.

- Allow them to make important choices and to live with the consequences of those choices.

- Honor their good efforts on constructive endeavors, whether they succeed or fail.

The size of task a child will attempt—and whether or not he will see it through—increases if he has already been allowed to attempt tasks he might not be able to finish, and if his failures (following good efforts) have been praised.

ASK YOURSELF

What did my parents do best?

How can I show my kids examples of lives worth copying?

SERIES G: Topic 6

Guiding Your Kids

Many parents would be horrified to hear this, including many who are guilty. The average parents spend less than 7 minutes a week talking to their children, according to an article that appeared in *USA Today*.

Spend time every day with each of your children doing things they like to do. While doing so, avoid serious topics, issues, and questions unless your child brings them up. Comment favorably on as many things about your child as you can.

Children become competent when the power they receive is won by being responsible and making good decisions. Children who get too much power too soon tend to misuse it.

Exerting too much control can cause children to withdraw from life, rebel or become bullies. On the other hand, permissiveness encourages youngsters to push parents to the limit of their tolerance. It allows children to think everything revolves around their own wishes. It causes children to demand undeserved rewards and to fail to appreciate the advantages they have.

Except when a child has a specific need like hunger or a diaper change, his behavior is a negotiation. Everything he does has a purpose. A child's misbehavior can become his way of gaining:

- Power or the ability to do whatever he wants (often learned from parents who are bossy).

- Attention from parents who put up with tantrums, or who have to constantly remind, punish, reward, coax or cater to a child.

- Revenge by being difficult and making your life harder, to punish you for not letting him have his own way (often learned from parents who retaliate).

Children do what works. Misbehavior is reinforced when parents don't draw clear boundaries or confront the negative behaviors.

Crying is your child's way of negotiating. In families where both parents are deaf, their children cry much less because crying simply doesn't work. A child who is used to having free reign will test his parent's resolve by behaving more forcefully until the adult either gives up or reclaims his control of the child.

When you react to children's misbehavior in a way that puts you in a bad light or makes your reaction predictable, they can do that to you all the time just to entertain themselves. You become their puppet.

Misbehavior needs to be met in a way that is calm. Give your child simple commands that you enforce. State consequences clearly and firmly and enforce them always, especially if your child is testing you. Briefly explain the rules. State them only once. Do not feel like you need to defend them. You are not in a debate. Be a parent, not a pal.

When your child can make you react, you give them power over you and reward bad behavior.

If your child misbehaves, it's often because you have given him an immediate reward for doing so: the power to control you. When you make a rule or a decision, explaining your reasoning helps him make good explanations. But when he can make you give him an explanation over and over, he is turning you into his fool. When your child uses his antics or behavior to dictate the terms of your parenting, you have to break up the reinforcement process by reacting to him or her in new ways. You have to make sure his attempts to manipulate you don't work. Enforce your rules and commands. Respond to him when you want, not while he is using his routine on you. Maybe you'll choose not to respond at all.

> **Studies have found children feel more self-assured when they have been given clearly established rules and family structure with the parents firmly in charge.**

Giving in to children too often leads to disrespect. Parents who are overly helpful prevent their children from learning to think on their feet. Don't interfere too much with your children as they attempt things that are at the upper limit of their capabilities (or that have an element of danger). Struggling and overcoming helps develop character. Self-esteem requires coping skills, and those skills are best learned when children are allowed to solve their own problems and deal with the consequences.

Children are quite skillful at driving wedges between parents. Children can't "divide and conquer" unless their parents let them; agree in advance to back each other up.

ASK YOURSELF

How have I been letting my children take power from me?

How can I keep an or Johnnie or Ann challenged?

Empowering Your Kids

Children are empowered when they know:

- They are capable.
- They are loved.
- They are in charge of their lives.
- They have your support to go after their goals.
- They are trusted to responsibly use the resources you make available to them.
- Whether they succeed or fail, their reasonable efforts will be honored and appreciated.
- Neither their successes nor their failures will change their worth as a person in good standing in the family unless their misbehavior is willful.

> **Children make good judgments sooner when they have been allowed to "color outside the lines," and when they have been allowed to experience the consequences of their decisions.**

When you applaud their genuine efforts—even if those efforts fail—you encourage them to persist and to attempt more difficult undertakings. Parents who allow their children to take a wholesome path that is different or less efficient than their own are demonstrating faith in their children's ability to find their own way, which gives youngsters self-confidence.

**Never pass up a chance to praise your children
when their way turns out to be better than yours.**

If there is a difference in opinions, ask your child to explain his views or share what's troubling him. Stay calm and discuss your position. Assure him you want to help, no matter what the problem is, and nothing he says will cause you to be outraged or turn on him. Go out of your way to approve as much of his thinking as possible.

Discipline

How much latitude you give your children is one of the hardest calls to make. No matter where you draw the line, they will think— and tell you—that you are being too controlling. In spite of their protests, children prefer clarity and strict rules over permissive-ness or nagging. Stay kind, clear and firm. State your expectations and stick to them!

**Be careful not to reward bad behavior by
overreacting to it.**

It is easy for well-meaning parents to allow their children to "push their buttons" and run all over them.

Set age-appropriate boundaries and consequences for your chil-dren. Take an active part in all their pursuits. Be involved in their lives so you can verify the wholesomeness of their friends and activities. Be aware that you could become their problem if you schedule too many activities for them, or if you need them to excel for you to be happy. Leading is better than pushing your children. Pushing turns to criticism quickly, so if you have to do it, do it cleverly and as infrequently as possible.

Thoughts on How to Parent

The relationship you have with your child has more power to change him than the correctness or logic of your arguments.

Inside every child who is misbehaving is one who would be doing something constructive if he knew what it was or how he could get involved.

The sooner you become a good parent the better because the media and your children's peers are gaining power over children at increasingly younger ages.

When you lose your relationship, you lose your power.

When anger, defiance and the silent treatment don't work, with-holding your love seems like all there is left. Actually, withholding love is a very weak strategy. Acting distant from your child trains him to act distant from you. When you are distant, you lose more power. Look at how you got to where you are for ways to get you where you want to be.

When you withhold your love, your child is likely to seek it in the ways you fear most.

Rules of Thumb

Before and after every serious correction, reassure your child so he knows that the matter isn't enough to change your relationship.

- Be calm; having your emotional volume too high too often is useless, harmful and self-indulgent, and it shows a lack of parenting skills.
- You can be part of or maybe all of the problem.
- "They're doing what they're doing because you are doing what you are doing," according to Dr. Phil.

- Since you are the only one you can change, change others by fixing yourself. (See more on fixing in Topic F-4 at GetLifeRight. com.)

- Being involved and proactive in your children's lives is essential. To paraphrase President Ronald Reagan, no matter how much you trust them, it is essential to verify.

- Adults at a rehab facility recovering from addictions were asked how they got hooked. The most common answer was "My peers, and lack of parental knowledge and oversight when I was young. I was too far gone before they were aware of my condition." The answer was the same, whether these people thought they came from good homes or bad homes.

- Children should not be able to make their own rules until they are paying all their own bills.

- Misbehavior is a breach of your relationship.

- When your child's peers have more power over him than your closeness does, their vices have more power over him than your virtues do.

- Some children misbehave to get the love or attention they crave.

ASK YOURSELF

How can I get my child interested in activities that are more wholesome and appealing to him than misbehaving with his peers?

Craft the Best Life Possible

*Change your thinking,
change your life.*

SERIES H: Topic 1

Use Your Full Potential

Everything you think and do, moment by moment, increases or decreases your potential. Your lifetime potential is the total of all your thoughts and deeds, plus the value of all the good that results from them. It is the most you can achieve using your best thinking and all your energy all the time.

Few people come close to knowing and using all they are capable of. Since you can never know the future, you can never know the outer limits of what you can do.

Even if you seem to be getting through life quite well, you can still be falling far short of your potential.

While others may judge you by what you accomplish, what really counts is the quality of your efforts, more than the results of your efforts.

As you approach your potential in any area of your life, you experience an increase in pride, self-satisfaction and options. Just as your view of the world expands as you approach the horizon, the world of possibilities expands ahead of you. The possibilities that come into view create the excitement that takes the work out of getting ahead. The more you strive to reach your potential, the more likely you are to have moments that will take your breath away.

No matter what has held you back in your past, nothing is keeping you from becoming all you can be in the future.

Very small decisions can change your direction in life. A change of one degree can get a hiker lost by 100 feet for every mile he travels. You need a compass you can check with often. Your compass is your Plan.

You check your Plan by asking good questions. "How can I make the most important contribution?" "How can I position myself so I can be discovered?" "How can I observe experts doing what I want to be able to do?" "How can I improve my Plan for life?" "How can I keep from getting lost?"

Ways to use more of your potential:

- Use your time on the tasks that will produce the most lasting benefits and advantages for your future.

- Stop doing what doesn't work or is of little value.

- Work with others to accomplish tasks beyond what you could accomplish alone.

- Reduce the number of mistakes you make by learning more before you make important decisions.

- Maintain good relationships and seek new ones with those who inspire you, share your values or can help you become all you want to be.

- Put distance between those who don't have your best interests at heart or who cause you to be less than your best.

- Maintain balance in your life. A history of correct decisions in one area of your life is rarely enough to offset failure in another.

- Make sure your efforts and behavior work to the good of all concerned.

- Learn from experts up front before you develop bad habits or damage the project you are attempting to master.

> **A person who appears to be doing poorly may be performing closer to the top of his potential than a highly successful person.**

With the statement that follows, you can turn your experiences, even bad ones, into assets. It changes the way you look at them.

> **Everything that has happened to me, good and bad, and everything I am or am not capable of doing, make me perfectly suited to accomplish something very important. When I find that, I will find contentment, fulfillment, and happiness.**

Remember you can never get to the point where you have nothing to give. Former drug dealers are often the only ones who can reach those who are still "using." Former gang members are often the only ones who can convince some kids to get off the street. Fathers who weren't there for their kids can be there for other people's kids who have been neglected. GIs who have had to kill enemy soldiers and are haunted by their memories may find comfort in helping other "wounded warriors." Star Parker was a notorious prostitute and welfare cheat who became a celebrity by using her experience to get the welfare laws changed. It is the job of all those on their death beds to encourage their caregivers, so they will be happy working with others who need care.

With the exception of our living descendants, what you produced with your life will be gone soon after you die. If you take anything with you, it will be the value of what you did for others. Many people will be completely unaware of whom, how, and how many people they have helped.

Givers earn a stake in the lives of those they help.

Soldiers' lives can be brief, but their lifetime potential includes the benefits of freedom enjoyed by every person they have defended.

Parents' lifetime potential includes some part of the successes and quality of life of each child they have raised.

Doctors get a stake in the lives of their patients, the residents they teach to become doctors, and everyone who enters the hospital they helped build.

Teachers who have taught their students to strive and believe in themselves continue to reap benefits from students they have taught, long after the teachers have forgotten their students' names.

Caregivers ease the lives of others, often with little thanks, and at the cost of their own freedom. By being on hand at critical moments, they have the potential to change the direction of a soul, rehabilitate, witness, encourage or convey thoughts that are very helpful to their patients and their families.

ASK YOURSELF

Where will my life end up if I continue to do what I am doing?

What percentage of my potential have I been using?

What is the greatest gift I can make with my life?

Do I now see my life as being more valuable than I did?

What can I do that will keep giving after I am gone?

SERIES H: Topic 2

Make All Your Time Precious

Time is an asset, and so is your intellect. If you set out to do so, you can get more for your time; and if you invest that time in making yourself more valuable, your wealth will grow.

If a day had only 20 hours in it, you'd still get the important things done, just as you do now. What if, in that world, you could get 4 more hours if you wanted them badly enough to purchase them? The time you purchased would be precious to you. You would use it carefully for those things that would make the biggest difference in your life.

Well, those conditions already exist. When you use your 4 most precious hours of the day for ordinary tasks, you make your precious time ordinary time.

Your potential will skyrocket if you set aside your 4 precious hours to do those things that will make the biggest improvements in your life.

When you compress all of your other tasks into the hours that remain, it will make those hours more valuable.

Using Your Hours in Better Ways

For the pleasure of being alive, you use some fraction of every minute for existing; that is the part you "spend." You can "spend" the rest of that minute or you can "invest" it in things that will increase your capabilities and produce lasting value for yourself or others. *Note:* The word *spend* means to use up. All you have to show for it is a memory! During all the time you invest, however, you are still living and enjoying life. For example, while you invest your time in earning a college degree, you are probably having at least as much fun as you would have spending your time. But what you learned in college will improve your circumstances for the rest of your life.

> **The abundance and stability of your future depends on the wealth you have accumulated in all forms.**

Adding Levels of Benefit

If you watch TV, you get a basic benefit. If you exercise while the program is on, you receive a second level of benefit. If you are also watching programs that are educational or informative, you get another level of benefit.

> **The time you give to a good cause isn't spent. It gives you a stake in the lives of those you help, so it too becomes an asset.**

Normal Activities Compared to Better Activities

Consuming Time	Investing Time
Snacking during commercials	Exercising during commercials
Going to a ball game	Going to a museum
Vacationing nearby	Vacationing in a foreign country
Reading tabloids	Reading *Popular Mechanics*
Doing repetitive work	Doing creative work
Spending money	Saving money
Watching a sport	Playing a sport
Watching sitcoms	News or Discovery on TV
Eating junk food	Eating good food
Playing video games	Learning online
Hanging out online	Doing homework online

Commonsense Ideas for Managing Your Time

During your most productive hours, work on the task that will make the biggest improvement in your life.

Try to use all your time to get some long-term benefit for yourself or someone else.

Settle any issue that is a threat to you, such as a traffic ticket, late homework, registration for next semester's classes, etc.

Find ways to do your required tasks in as little time as possible.

Do small tasks you can remove from your task list completely.

Keep your Plan and your task list current so they can help you stay on course and alert to what you will need, to be ready for your upcoming tasks.

Take frequent breaks and use them to keep organized, exercise, celebrate your progress or socialize.

For problems with procrastination, read *The Now Habit* by Neil Fiore (www.neilfiore.com).

Handle your most unpleasant task (like delivering bad news to your boss or a customer) early in the morning so the task doesn't make you anxious all day.

Instead of doing things for which you get paid once, do things you can get paid for thousands of times. Collect or sell copies of books, paintings, songs or inventions; or manufacture or market products other people have created. Earn interest.

If you are going to risk your time or money, do it while you are young so you have time to recover if something goes wrong.

If you are running a long-distance race, climbing the steepest part at the beginning makes the rest of the race downhill. If you put it off until the last minute, you will have to do it when your energy level is low.

The same strategy applies to your life. If you have children early, they will consume the time your career requires and what would have been your "nest egg." If you get your education, house and investments before you have kids, those things can be growing in value while you spend quality time with your kids.

ASK YOURSELF

Of all the things you did this week, which one produced the most lasting benefits?

SERIES H: Topic 3

Enhance Your Life with a Purpose

You are a gift to the world. How you share yourself is your purpose and the primary source of your self-esteem. You can have a purpose without giving it a thought. A youth who signs up for the military probably doesn't think of it as a purpose, but it is. A teacher who inspires her students and puts her heart and soul into her work has a purpose, whereas a teacher who is just OK has a job.

Often the best purpose is the one that comes to you naturally or that you are best suited for. If you cause someone to benefit by the way you listen or advise them, being a good friend may be the purpose you were meant to have.

> **Your purpose is one of the things that makes you the proudest. It is one of the first things people say about you when they describe you to others.**

You add meaning to your life and give it direction when you have a purpose.

A popular definition of a purpose is **to give of yourself to a cause that is greater than you.**

About helping others, Muhammad Ali commented, **"Service to God is the rent we pay for our room in the hereafter."**

Mahatma Gandhi told us to **"Be the change you want to see in the world."**

A purpose is not intended to drive you toward accomplishments, but it can help you make better use of your time. When you have a tragedy in your world, working on your purpose is a good way to work through the pain, to heal and to keep from wallowing in your misfortune. Personal tragedies have caused many people to find cures, get legislation passed, raise money, organize support groups or strive to prevent similar tragedies in other families. Mothers Against Drunk Driving (MADD) is such a result, as is Megan's Law, which alerts the public when a child is missing or abducted.

Many who have become involved with a cause have grown along with it. The cause has made them keep striving when they could have leveled out. Many of their talents and gifts would have gone undiscovered were it not for their cause.

It's never too late to find a purpose. While a man convicted of murder awaited his sentence in court, he grabbed the bailiff's gun and killed the bailiff and two others. Then he hijacked a car and killed its owner. When the car ran out of gas, he broke into a nearby house, where the lady inside talked to him about a book she had just read, Rick Warren's *The Purpose-Driven Life*. Realizing his life could still have a purpose (keeping others from making the same mistakes he did), he surrendered to police.

To make the best use of our time on earth, we have to make good use of all we have. When we keep our minds fully engaged and our bodies fit, we are likely to be rewarded with longer and better lives.

By making computer software usable, Bill Gates made one of the greatest contributions to mankind. Surely that was satisfying to him as it was unfolding, but when he was done, it was no longer enough. To continue to be satisfied, he created a foundation and funded it with billions of dollars to help individuals for generations to come.

> **The good we have already done is not as satisfying as the good we are in the process of doing. When our purpose is to use our time and talent as best we can, our work is never done.**

ASK YOURSELF

Whose purpose has benefited my life most?

How can I add meaning to my life?

In one sentence, what is my purpose?

The Best Tip

The talents you already have are all you need to make a very important contribution to the world. You don't need break-through ideas; but you do need to make sure the ideas you use are a good fit for you, your family and your future. By "acting as if" your potential is much bigger, better and more easily attainable, it will become so. You will grow into the future you envision and go after.

As you apply the lessons in this book to your life, you will:

• Better understand yourself, others and your situation.

• Be pleased by how well you are using your judgment and creativity to solve your problems and make the most of your opportunities.

• Feel the love and appreciation you are pouring into others, being returned to you.

Billions of people have found great peace, meaning and strength by believing in a power greater than themselves. That's why it's a key ingredient in many of the best known rehabilitation programs. It allows you to explain your situation and the things that happen to you, good and bad, in ways that help you cope, recover and make the most of your life.

Stay in touch with us at

GetLifeRight.com

About the Author

The ideas in this book helped Dave retire young and comfortable.

Dave struggled as a student. Stories of the Great Depression and the end of World War II made him frugal and focused. He followed the advice of several self-help books. He chose real estate, where judgment, common sense and a good plan were more valuable than "school smarts."

He turned his weaknesses into advantages:

- He overcame his timid nature by "acting as if" he had courage.

- He dealt with his dyslexia by attempting fewer things, staying organized, keeping his life simple and gathering more and better information before he made his decisions.

- Because he couldn't process as much information at one time as many of his competitors, Dave was cautious about the number of properties he could handle. As a result, he survived the three real estate recessions when many of his more capable competitors failed.

- To offset his anxiety, he exercised hard and often. By staying fit, he was able to ride dirt bikes over thousands of miles of fabulous trails in many parts of the world. At 70+, Dave runs the Great Silverado Foot Race and rides many of the most scenic and challenging mountain bike trails in the country.

For his profession, he work for companies that constructed buildings for retail chains and which would allow him to take most of his pay in partial ownership of the buildings. That gave him the highest long-term growth potential with the least risk. Twenty-five years later, with the mortgages paid off, the properties generate more cash flow every year.

His wife Dianne handled the kids and the house and kept their lives in balance. That allowed him to accumulate wealth, head a charity, and mentor youths and adults in prisons and halfway houses.

His joy is helping others increase their potential and enjoyment of life.

What Readers Are Saying

"This is an excellent source with motivating and inspiring anecdotes and profound wisdom keys."

~Tobin Crenshaw

"I'm making better use of my time now that I treat it as an asset, and I'm thinking so much more clearly now that I am requiring myself to do so."

~Alan Davis

"I want to be more emotionally stable and not let my circumstances throw me. This book talks about changing and having direction in your life. I've never had a plan for my life ... not really, because I never expect to live very long. But this has me working on one."

~Shelley

"This book will help many people breathe a sigh of relief because they will realize that there is something they can do to change their life around."

~ Cyrus Webb

"Acting like newlyweds!" Before we finished the relationship topics, we had stopped bickering and felt we could work through just any problem in the future.

~ Al & Louise

Ways to Get Life Right

Join us on Social Media (See our Tips weekly)

Twitter: @Get_Life_Right / https://twitter.com/get_life_right

Facebook: https://www.facebook.com/getliferight

Pinterest: https://www.pinterest.com/GetLifeRight/

YouTube: https://www.youtube.com/channel/
UCjclAphFmt7apKeqRmYoDzw
(Look for simplified version on our website soon)

Free Interactive Features at getliferight.com

Previews of Each Topic — Quickly find and review topics of importance to you.

Additional Topics Not in the Book — Check out the regularly added new content.

Skillful Thoughts — Common thoughts that limit you – changed to empower you

Place It Forward — Free books for special events or to leave where they can help others.

Search for comments, questions, articles, resources, input from readers and our recommendations by Topic (Example C-4)

Bulk — Special deals for professional, educational or charitable purposes.

Help a Friend — Some people who are very important to you could benefit from this book significantly. Gift a book to someone important to you or leave one where ti can positively impact a stranger.

CPSIA information can be obtained
at www.ICGtesting.com
Printed in the USA
FSOW03n1814261116
27726FS